The Pension Investment Guide

Robin Ellison and Adam Jolly

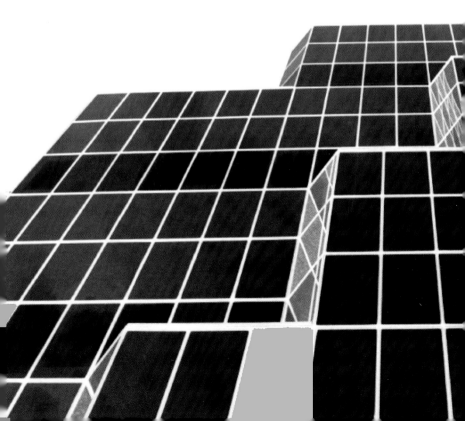

Thorogood Publishing Ltd 2008
10-12 Rivington Street
London EC2A 3DU

Telephone: 020 7749 4748
Fax: 020 7729 6110
Email: info@thorogoodpublishing.co.uk
Web: www.thorogoodpublishing.co.uk

Advertising sales negotiated by
Petersham Publishing Ltd
Petersham House
57A Hatton Garden
London EC1N 8JG

A catalogue record for this book is available from
the British Library

ISBN 1 85418 430 X
    978-185418430-6

Book typeset and designed in the UK
by Driftdesign

Printed in the UK by Ashford Colour Press Ltd

Foreword

It was never easy being a pension fund trustee; and the last few years have not made it any easier. In particular the demands of knowledge and understanding imposed by the Pensions Act 2004 have stretched the skills of many trustees, and even if they were up to speed on what the deed said, and how pension law worked, many found the investment side of trusteeship something of a challenge.

Investment issues had traditionally been secondary to benefit concerns. In any event, investment matters were traditionally delegated to asset managers and investment consultants. And the trustee knowledge requirements were broadly restricted to deciding how much to put in equities and how much in gilts.

The legal changes now make this insufficient. The need to establish statements of investment principles, the attempt to balance the investment objectives of members and of plan sponsors, the intervention of the law in proxy voting and in social and ethical investments – and the increasing interest in defined contribution systems – means that trustees, most of them investment laymen, are now centre stage in making informed financial decisions to cover a scheme's future liabilities and to manage their risks in a way in which they can be held to account. At the same time, they are having to consider more complex and innovative financial instruments to diversify their portfolios and to improve their returns.

This book is designed as a practical, easy-to-follow guide to the new financial environment in which pension trustees are having to learn to operate. In allocating assets, the book considers the pros and cons of traditional asset classes, such as equities, bonds, property and cash, and it examines the potential for (and risks of) investing in less conventional asset classes, such as hedge funds, private equity, commodities and infrastructure, where the rewards can be high – as can the pitfalls. It covers the issues facing not only trustees of defined benefit schemes but also those of the fast-developing defined contribution arrangements.

It also explores the use of innovative financial instruments, such as futures, swaps and options, explaining what they are and how they may help pension funds of all sizes invest where appropriate in a more efficient and flexible manner. It also attempts to give a balanced view, not always advanced by the sales departments of investment banks, of some of the drawbacks of such products.

And in the light of the need to design and follow the statement of investment principles, ensure the employer's covenant is strong enough to cover any deficits, meet the statutory funding objective and agree a schedule of contributions the book concludes by discussing some of the latest strategies that trustees might pursue in improving their returns and limiting their risks.

For trustees, especially lay trustees, the task of making these apparently investment decisions can appear intimidating or intoxicating. But it is manageable. First, the legal obligations are tempered by proportionality; no-one expects the smaller schemes to have the knowledge and expertise or resources of the larger ones. Second, even the smaller firms of advisers now have sufficient back-up to help guide

NOTES

trustees through much of the latest investment thinking and techniques. Third, a healthy circumspection will keep trustees from some of the more esoteric products marketed by some of the banks. It is not unreasonable to adopt a rule of thumb that if you do not understand what you are investing in, you might want to think twice about putting money in.

It is also wise to take it easy when following fashions in investment. It is currently argued by many observers, for instance, that assets should match your liabilities, and that pension obligations are 'bond-like'; but adopting a bond-like investment strategy may have risks of its own – and only be achievable at disproportionate expense. This book should help even trustees of smaller schemes, even if not all of the content applies to those particular circumstances. Its aim is to help you think through the principles on which you are investing your assets, not be intimated by much of the jargon – and ask the right questions of your advisors. The trustee role is a non-executive one – and to ensure your advisers help you get the best long-term deal you can for your members without excessive charges or exposure to too high a risk.

The speed and scale at which investment strategies and techniques have been developing in the last ten years is great; but the basic principles remain as valid as ever, and there is rarely any magic formula for increasing return, lowering risk and controlling expenses.

In any event financial and economic circumstances almost always change too rapidly for any particular set of investment assumptions or solutions to last too long. One of the major dangers is being locked into a novel investment product which may be suitable for one set of circumstances but which may not work when those circumstances change. And since few can anticipate just how those circumstances can change, investment flexibility, even for mature schemes, can be critical.

So the standard nostrums still apply; diversification, understanding what the investments are, realistic objectives, sensible advisers and asset managers who are given some room to use their skills.

We very much hope that trustees will find this book a readable, sensible, balanced and jargon-free guide to pension fund investment – even if you have no previous experience of investment at all. You should find it helpful as much by browsing its pages as by reading it right through. And given time, a fair wind, and decent advisers you and your 750,000 pension trustee colleagues in the UK should be able make a major contribution to improving the level and security of your members' retirement income.

Robin Ellison
Adam Jolly

NOTES

Over the last five years, we've brought back some impressive *Institutional* PROFITS.

Again.

And again.

And again.

Some Artemis Institutional Profit hunters are characterised by their stealth, cunning and patience. Others by their derring-do. There is one attribute, however, that they all share in common. They're consistent. A glance at the table below reveals that our aces have been bagging monster Profits year in, year out. In each and every region of the Institutional landscape.

This is by no means a coincidence. It's a direct result of the Artemis hunting approach. You see, unlike more straight-laced outfits, the Artemis aces are given leave to follow their instincts, wherever they may lead. Leaving them free to adapt to prevailing economic conditions. Or to act on their convictions. Using tactics learned from years of hunting Profits across the world. But with the added support of a dedicated Institutional back up team. If you'd like to find out more about how to bag Institutional Profits – again and again and again – why not call Elaine Gordon or Benita Kaur on 020 7399 6000. E-mail them at institutionalteam@artemisfunds.com. Or alternatively check out our website www.artemisonline.co.uk for details.

Institutional Strategy	Relative outperformance per annum*		
	1 year%	3 years%	5 years%
EQUITY INCOME	4.43	2.76	3.95
UK GROWTH	4.63	2.02	6.04
UK SPECIAL SITUATIONS	7.00	4.61	7.83
UK ALPHA	3.76	3.88	–
GLOBAL CAPITAL	14.71	16.03	–
EUROPEAN GROWTH	2.08	5.02	7.40

*To the Funds' Benchmark

ARTEMIS
The PROFIT Hunter

Mutual respect. Organic growth. Intellectual curiosity. Apparently it's why we're different.

www.pictet.com
Private Banking
Independent Asset
Managers
Family Office
Global Custody
Asset Management
Investment Funds

Geneva Zurich London Tokyo
Luxembourg Nassau Singapore Lausanne
Paris Frankfurt Madrid Milan Turin
Florence Rome Montreal Hong Kong

PICTET

1805

Independent minds

NOTES

Contents

Looking for pension scheme performance?

Société Générale Asset Management:

- A specialist fund management house
- The backing of the third largest asset management company in the Eurozone
- Group worldwide assets of £252bn (at March 2007)
- UK equity high alpha expertise
- Comprehensive investment approach
- Investment access to all major geographic markets and asset classes

Contact: Tessa Kohn-Speyer

📞 020 7090 2635

📧 marketing@sgam.co.uk

🖥 www.sgam.co.uk

UK Equities | European Equities
US Equities | Emerging Markets Equities
Japanese Equities | Global Equities
UK Bonds | International Bonds

 SOCIETE GENERALE
Asset Management

Issued by Société Générale Asset Management UK Limited (authorised and regulated by the Financial Services Authority) trading as Société Générale Asset Management. For your security, any calls may be recorded and randomly monitored. Past performance is not a guide to future performance. The price of shares may go down as well as up and you may not get back the amount originally invested. Exchange rate fluctuations may cause the value of underlying overseas investments to go up or down.

NOTES

NOTES

NOTES

HYMANS ROBERTSON

Stephen Birch
Head of Manager Research and
enthusiastic bagpipe player

**Finely tuned investment advice
from the leading independent experts
in investments and benefits.**

At Hymans Robertson we have some unique qualities to offer.

- We give genuinely tailored advice specific for your requirements
- We have a unique manager research offering which gives maximum flexibility for our clients
- Our market leading strategy team provide innovative solutions for our clients

And just in case you need any more convincing, we were the winner of Global Money Management's Consultant of the Year Award 2007.

London | Glasgow | Birmingham

For more information please contact marketing@hymans.co.uk or visit www.hymans.co.uk

Real people. Real skills. Real results.

The issues facing trustees

Gail Paterson, Partner, Hymans Robertson

They may be largely unpaid volunteers, but pension fund trustees are becoming increasingly more powerful figures. Trustees have played a key role in several recent corporate restructurings, as their position on scheme funding can be crucial in determining the success of take-overs or private equity buy-outs. Despite this, relatively little is known about trustees and their views about their work.

To find out more about what trustees are thinking, Hymans Robertson, with the help of *Engaged Investor* magazine, carried out a major survey of trustee attitudes and views. The results, from 157 trustees, give an invaluable insight into the work of a small group of dedicated people who act on behalf of millions of pension scheme members.

Key concerns

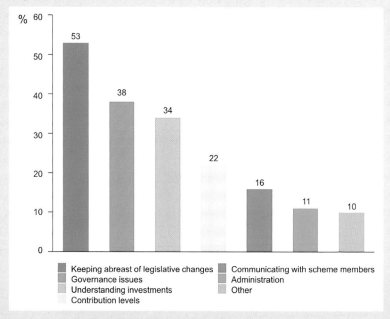

We asked trustees to select the two most significant areas of challenge for them. Unsurprisingly, keeping up to date with legislation was seen as the biggest challenge for trustees (53% of respondents), while its complexity was the most likely issue to keep them awake at night. These results suggest that government attempts to simplify pension legislation still have a considerable way to go and that trustees are still getting to grips with the new regulatory regime.

Governance, or the overall running of a scheme, and understanding investment were also seen as important challenges. Contribution levels, communicating with scheme members and administration scored less highly. This may reflect trustees' beliefs that these areas of scheme operation are straightforward enough to run efficiently with little trustee intervention, but we suspect that it is more likely to be a result of the trustees' only having time to focus their attention on the top-rated areas.

Trustee skills

In terms of their work, trustees see decision-making and communication skills as the most important attributes. At the same time, awareness of governance issues followed by knowledge of finance and investment were given as the strengths that trustees feel they possess for the role. Trustees need to be able to decide on a course of action after discussing it among themselves and hearing the views of their advisers. The results reflect this, although some will be concerned that they do not have more financial and investment knowledge.

Is trusteeship unpopular?

One surprising finding was that, despite the problems they face and the need for considerable time commitment, almost three-quarters of trustees said they would recommend the role to others with similar experience and expertise and less than 10% would not recommend it. Despite the negative press for pensions, and indeed trusteeship, the fact that so many trustees would recommend the job suggests things are not as black as sometimes painted.

There was also evidence that trustees don't feel appreciated, as a little over half of those who expressed an opinion think they should be paid, with many saying this would recognise the vital work that they do. It is interesting to see a majority of trustees, but not an overwhelming one, approving of payment for their work. The increasing amount of time for training may be causing this, along with a feeling that their work is often under-appreciated.

Member understanding

The survey highlighted a possible concern for employers, as most trustees think that scheme members don't fully understand their pension scheme. The average trustee thought that only 29% of their scheme members had a good understanding of the scheme. This figure breaks down as 30% for defined benefit schemes, 39% for DC schemes and, perhaps unsurprisingly, 20% for the more complex hybrid schemes.

Time spent dealing with legislative and regulatory issues may be preventing trustees from spending more time on communications with members.

Diversity

The survey found three significant groups for trustees' career backgrounds; financial services (31%), administration (15%) and accountancy (13%). Other backgrounds, such as legal, teacher, media, IT, engineering and health professional had a low representation among respondents, 5% or less.

Finally, the survey raises the question of whether trustee boards are sufficiently diverse, as it found that the typical trustee is likely to be a man aged 50 or over and living in London or the South East. It is a concern that there is not more representation of women and younger age groups among trustees. The geographic bias to London and the South East could be a reflection of the fact that many company head offices are located in this region.

Paul Myners has, before now, queried whether pension schemes can operate efficiently with non-professional trustees. Our survey identifies that these dedicated individuals are doing very well to address the issues that confront them, and that it is premature to write them off.

Asked to identify two features of their work that motivated them to be a trustee, 67% mentioned the protection of members' interests, and 54% said that they wanted to ensure that the scheme is run effectively. Fewer said that they were trustees because they found the work interesting, or because they enjoyed exercising their financial or investment knowledge.

In conclusion, trustees have an increasingly powerful and pivotal role within the UK corporate world, but the pressures put on them through complex legislation and governance issues do make the role challenging. However, despite this environment, trustees are motivated by the role and would encourage others to get involved; good news for members and good news for companies.

For more information or to request a full copy of the survey *Issues Facing Trustees 2007*, please contact:

Tel: +44 (0)20 7082 6197
Email: lucy.steers@hymans.co.uk

Alternatively, visit www.hymans.co.uk to find out more.

HYMANS ROBERTSON

Part 1

The trustee as investor

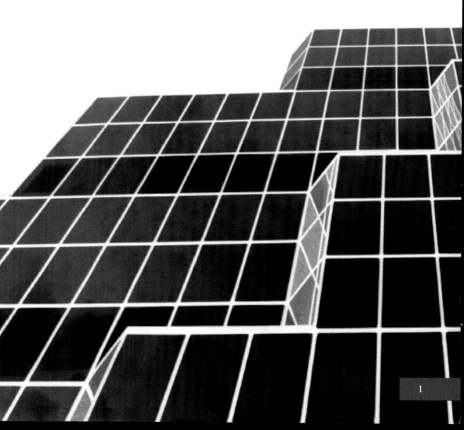

Chapter 1
The trustee's role

In the last decade, the role of managing a workplace pension as a trustee has become more tightly defined and more complex. A series of regulatory changes has unambiguously placed responsibility on them for making strategic investment decisions on behalf of their members. At the same time, the cosy assumptions on which asset allocation once depended are being broken. It is no longer enough to settle for annual returns benchmarked against everyone else.

To meet future liabilities and achieve higher returns, trustees are routinely having to consider alternative assets, notably private equity and hedge funds, which demand a new way of thinking about investment returns. At the same time, they are having to explore how they can use derivatives to match their assets and liabilities more efficiently without exposing themselves to a total loss of their capital.

Although trustees are non-executives, relying on professional advice and delegating day-to-day investment decisions, they now have to be sure that they are in a position to ask some searching questions about the basis on which their funds are being invested. Should they abandon bonds altogether in the search for higher returns in privately held assets? Or should they tie the future flow of payments to their members to a predictable stream of income? How trustees respond will have far-reaching implications for the future benefits of their members.

Trust and regulation

Most workplace pensions in the UK have traditionally been set up as trusts to separate the interests of the sponsoring company and the people who benefit. As a trustee, your job is to act on behalf of the beneficiaries.

Your actions are governed by a deed, which gives you a series of powers. The strength of these varies from scheme to scheme, but will include the right and obligation to set the investment strategy for funds contributed to the scheme.

Until the late 1990s, despite what the law actually said, pension funds in the UK were largely unrestricted in making their investments. In the 1920s, Parliament had placed severe limits on trustees. Only the safest investments were allowed. But it was a fall-back position. In practice, trustees were nearly always granted wide extra powers under their deeds.

The Pensions Act of 1995 addressed this anomaly. The power of trustees to invest was enshrined in law. You can now buy anything, as long as you take proper advice and act as if you are looking after money for other people.

In return for bringing the law up to date, however, all trusts now fall under the supervision of a Pensions Regulator, who has responsibility for monitoring the level of risk in all schemes.

Knowledge and understanding

The main consequence for trustees of this new regulatory regime is that you are now formally expected to have 'knowledge and understanding' of the law relating to pensions and trusts, as well as the principles relating to the funding of occupational schemes and to the investment of assets. Within six months, you must know enough to be able to perform your role in a way that satisfies the regulator.

Behind this requirement lies the objective of freeing trustees from the herd mentality in financial markets by putting them in a position to make informed, independent and active decisions about setting an investment strategy designed specifically around the needs of their scheme.

As a trustee that means that you are going to have to complete three particular tasks: develop a clear view of how your scheme is going to meet its future liabilities, work out your investment principles and decide how to allocate your assets.

What impacts our investment decisions?

Invesco Perpetual looks at the impact psychological factors have on our investment decisions

'Behavioural finance' applies findings from psychological research to finance to enable us to better understand and explain why we make certain financial decisions.

Academics studying behavioural finance have found that individuals do not always make rational investment decisions and they have identified a number of areas where psychology has tended to lead investors to make irrational decisions.

Look to the long-term

One of behavioural finance's key findings is that investors place a far higher significance on losses than gains. Research shows that individuals put a worth on losses that is two and a half times the worth they ascribe to gains*. This finding has been used to explain the equity risk premium – one of the basic justifications of equity investing – which basically says that over the long-term equities have on average outperformed bonds.

According to the Barclays Capital Equity Gilt Study 2006, over the past 106 years to 31 December 2005, equities have outperformed gilts by 4% a year. Yet, in the short term, the greater volatility of equities compared to bonds means there is a greater chance of making short-term losses. The aversion to investment losses, together with a tendency for short-term investing, means investors are often guilty of not giving equities valuations as high as they otherwise might have.

Behavioural finance research indicates that we should have the mindset of long-term investors and be willing to invest with at least five to ten-year time horizons in mind, or even longer, if possible.

Take a holistic approach

A further finding of behavioural finance is that the framing of financial questions has a bearing on the answers reached. In practical terms, the most common implication of this is that financial decisions are often viewed in isolation when they should be viewed together.

For example, people tend to consider their current accounts, deposit accounts, investment funds, credit cards and mortgages separately. Generally speaking, however, it would be far better financially to think of

them together. For example, it is generally better to pay off debt with a credit balance than to pay out a certain rate of interest on the debt and collect a rather smaller one on the credit.

By taking a holistic approach to financial arrangements, people would be able to evaluate all their assets and liabilities together and avoid an unnecessary segregation of accounts.

Don't get sucked into momentum-driven rallies

A final important observation of behavioural finance is that investors often under or over-react to stockmarket information. The most notable recent example of this was the 'dot com' bubble, when stock prices greatly exceeded reasonable valuations.

Investors often use a limited set of information, which they regard as representative, when reaching decisions. For example, companies may be regarded as 'winners' or 'losers' depending on recent stock market performance. This tag may give a stock price momentum in one direction or another for long after this is justified, which could have a similar effect on the whole stock market.

In conclusion

Overall behavioural finance opposes what is often referred to as 'rational finance', which sees financial decisions being made in the context of a rational appraisal of risk and return. In particular, it further stresses the importance of investing for the long-term and having a tolerance for short-term losses. Research into investor psychology identifies observable and systematic errors in the decisions which are made by investors and the recognition of these may help in making better financial decisions.

Further information

For further information on key investment topics, visit Invesco Perpetual's website dedicated to pension scheme trustees at:
www.trusteetraining.co.uk

Invesco Perpetual UK Institutional team
Tel: 0207 065 3489
www.invescoperpetual.co.uk/institutional

Invesco
Perpetual

When making pension investments, you need a company that's rock-solid and has stood the test of time. Now, about that mountain logo.

Making a big decision on behalf of a company's entire workforce is something you need to be sure about. You need to speak to an investment company with stability. Our fund managers tend to stick with us longer. We have more fund managers with 10-year plus track records than any other group in the UK†. We believe this is good for us as well as for our clients. Should you want to look your fund manager up in a few years' time, chances are he or she won't have moved on to the next job.

The long-term welfare of a lot of employees, both past and present, is at stake. Speak to the people who are known for their long-term vision. The one with the particularly relevant mountain logo.

020 7065 3041
invescoperpetual.co.uk/institutional

Chapter 2
Scheme funding

As a trustee, your main concern is to ensure that your members' benefits are going to be properly funded and protected. As far as possible, you want to be sure that pensions are going to be paid now and into the future.

Since 2005, this obligation has been encapsulated by the Pension Regulator as the 'statutory funding objective'. Essentially, you are going to have to demonstrate that you have sufficient assets to meet any 'technical provisions'. Or, in other words, are you actually going to be able to fulfil your ongoing commitment to pay benefits to current and future pensioners?

Predicting your liabilities so far into the future with any certainty is a hazardous business, particularly as people are living longer and you do not know by how much rates of pay are going to change in the next 5, 10 or 20 years.

In consultation with an actuary (a specialist who advises you on your long-term liabilities), you are responsible for drawing up a valuation of the scheme as the basis for judging whether the current level of funding is going to be sufficient.

You will then have to agree your conclusions with your sponsoring employer. Such discussions are bound to be sensitive. Employers naturally want to keep their contributions down and are prone to taking a rosy view of the potential upside on any investments. You will tend to be more cautious and prefer to keep contributions up.

But when a shortfall is identified in funding members' benefits, negotiations on how to cover the deficit can become difficult, particularly as the Pensions Regulator is encouraging trustees to think like bankers in such situations. The line is that any deficit should be treated like a default on a loan.

Given that the collective deficit on UK pensions was at one time estimated to have reached as much as £700bn, most trustees now find themselves with a demanding extra dimension to their role. Where there is a deficit, you are responsible for drawing up a recovery plan under the supervision of the Pensions Regulator, which necessitates taking a more aggressive stance in pressing employers for extra contributions.

In the worst case, depending on your powers under the deed, you might even have to ask for the scheme to be wound up and for the employer to settle all current and future liabilities now.

The valuation

Long before any such drastic action may be necessary, trustees are expected to conduct a regular valuation to check whether their statutory funding objective is being met or not. Under your direction, an actuary will undertake the technical work and advise you on what assumptions to make in deciding on your valuation.

On likely investment returns, you want to see a range of outcomes and are expected by the Pensions Regulator to take a 'prudent view'. You should check too whether the rate for calculating your liabilities is linked to UK government securities or is set at a higher level by the actuary. The effect on the extent of your liabilities can be dramatic.

You also need to consider carefully assumptions about mortality and how longer life expectancy actually applies to your members. Where in the country are they based? What type of work have they undertaken? Any variations should be checked, as they can be significant.

The sponsoring employer

The valuation can no longer be made without taking account of the position of the sponsoring employer. As a trustee, you are expected to examine closely its financial position and ask whether it can continue to fund the scheme if the current investment strategy falls short of expectations.

Employers are now obliged to supply you with any information you might reasonably require about how its business is performing and in the event of any transaction, such as an acquisition, disposal or restructuring, you can expect to be closely involved.

The recovery plan

If the pension fund is showing a deficit, then trustees are expected by the Pensions Regulator to find ways of eliminating it as swiftly as the employer can reasonably afford. In practice that means conducting any negotiations on extra funding while taking into account an employer's business plan, planned investments and patterns of expenditure. You can then take a view on whether to ask for:

- a one-off payment to balance the books

- an increase in the level of monthly contributions
- an adjustment in the retirement age

The approach that you take will be coloured by the age profile of your members. If many have already retired, then a one-off payment is likely to be preferable. If, instead, most are going to be working for years to come, then contributions can be pushed up over a longer period.

In your back pocket, it is worth knowing your chances of pursuing an employer to make good any deficiency in the event of winding up a scheme.

If you fail to reach agreement with your employer on contributions, then you can ask the Pensions Regulator for guidance.

Schedule of contributions

Trustees can now fulfil one of their most important responsibilities: making sure the right money is paid into the scheme at the right time. In 'a schedule of contributions', which has to be approved by your actuary to take effect, you should specify what employers and employees are going to pay into the scheme and when.

You should make clear in the document exactly what rates apply, rather than referring to any other paperwork, and employers have to pay in employees' contributions 19 days from the end of the month of their pay being deducted.

Trustees are charged to make sure the contributions are right and on time. If late payments start to threaten the security of members' benefits, then the Pension Regulator should be notified.

NOTES

Funding statements

Fifteen months after conducting a valuation, as a trustee you have to agree 'a statement of funding principles' with your sponsoring employer, in which all the assumptions used in calculating the balance of liabilities and assets are explained. You should also spell out the basis on which any deficit is going to be covered.

However, within three months of a valuation, 'a summary funding statement' should be sent to members of the scheme, in which you explain any changes to the funding position of the scheme.

opdu

Protecting Pension Funds

opdu protects pension funds by providing unique insurance cover to trustees, administrators and sponsoring employers. Pension funds holding total combined assets in excess of £115 billion have joined **opdu**. The membership ranges from large funds to small.

opdu's members can readily purchase limits of cover between £1 million and £30 million. **opdu's** cover has been developed for the special insurance needs of pension funds but can be varied to meet the specific requirements of individual schemes.

opdu affords a valuable external resource for reimbursing losses suffered by pension funds. The asset protection thereby given is ultimately of benefit to pension fund members.

Key Benefits

opdu provides a unique combination of risk management and comprehensive insurance:

To	For
Trustees	Errors and omissions
Corporate trustees	TPR civil fines and penalties
Directors of corporate trustees	Ombudsman complaints
Sponsoring employers	Defence costs
The pension fund	Employer indemnities
Internal administrators	Exonerated losses
Internal advisers	Litigation costs
Internal dispute managers	Retirement cover - 12 years

Advisory Service

- Problem solving
- Guidance on minimising liabilities
- Personal representation
- Working with your own advisers

Litigation Costs Extension is also available to give increased protection to pension fund assets. The cover is able to pay the legal costs and expenses incurred by trustees or ordered to be paid out of the pension fund in seeking a declaration or directions from the court.

psb

The Challenge for Pension Funds

- To be fully funded within **10 years**
- Without becoming over funded
- Avoiding trapped surpluses

The Solution

The Pension Support Bond
- Cost effective and flexible
- Minimises exposure to over-funding
- Maintains the quality of your commitment to your pension scheme
- A Bermuda Segregated Account structure

Flexibility

- Size and timing of contributions
- Valued as a pension scheme asset up to level of deficit
- Choice of trigger points for pay-out
- Investment freedom
- Surplus to sponsor

A capital redemption bond providing security for pension funds while preserving assets for sponsoring employers

opdu
P E N S I O N
S U P P O R T
B O N D

For the full details please contact Jonathan Bull at opdu:
Tel 020 7204 2432   Fax 020 7204 2477   Email jonathan.bull@opdu.com
www.opdu.com

THE OCCUPATIONAL PENSIONS DEFENCE UNION LIMITED
International House   26 Creechurch Lane   London EC3A 5BA

Trapped surpluses: managing deficits

Jonathan Bull, Executive Director, opdu Ltd

A pension support bond

Pension deficits still make headlines. There is no complete solution to enable employers to eradicate deficits and avoid future exposure to pension risk. Even schemes that today appear to be fully-funded may produce deficits in the future. Employers have to make difficult decisions as to the appropriate level of funding to maintain schemes and clear deficits. Many employers, while wholly committed to funding their pension schemes, are now becoming worried about the risk of over-funding as a result of responding to pressure to fund using relatively short-term valuation criteria.

If an employer is worried about over-funding its pension scheme while the pension trustees are simultaneously maintaining pressure for early eradication or added security in a recovery plan, a Pension Support Bond may be of interest to both parties. The Pension Support Bond is a new product developed in consultation with **opdu** specifically to give added security while removing the risk of over-funding.

The Pension Support Bond works in a similar manner to an escrow account but without some of the drawbacks normally associated with contingent assets. It is structured as a long-term insurance policy. Pension contributions by the employer to fund the premiums for the Bond are tax deductible. The value of the policy will be a pension scheme asset through the period of a recovery plan. When the policy is surrendered at the end of the recovery plan, the surplus after clearing any residual deficit will revert to the employer – thus avoiding over-funding.

Whenever there is a potential prospect of over-funding during the course of a recovery plan, employers may wish to consider such a solution in order to achieve a fair balance of interests between their shareholders and their pension scheme members.

For more information please contact:
Tel: 020 7204 2432

Alternatively, visit www.opdu.com to find out more.

Chapter 3
Powers to invest

Until the late 1990s, trustees were free to take decisions without having to take into account too much legislation. Today, your behaviour and choices as an investor are subject to more scrutiny and control, following the Pensions Acts (1995 and 2004).

You have wide powers to invest, acting as if the assets in the scheme were your own. That does not mean chancing your arm. You should only take on as much risk as you would if, for instance, you were setting aside funds for a member of your family.

Suitable care

You are now formally expected to exercise 'reasonable care' in selecting investments that are suitable to meet the future liabilities of your scheme and the particular needs of your different members. You have to consider any potential risks and spread your investments between different types of assets.

In effect, there are two kinds of diversification. As well as striking a balance between equities, bonds and property within a portfolio, you have to make sure that each of these assets has a proper spread. In particular, if you decide to invest in UK equities only, then you could find yourself over-reliant on three or four major corporations which account for close to half of the value of the FTSE 100 index of leading companies. There is an argument for investing locally, but asset managers will ask you not to set too restrictive a mandate.

In short, the goal is to act 'prudently'. As a trustee, your priority is to safeguard the security, quality and liquidity of your scheme. In the case of a shortfall, you will find yourself having to stick closely to the statutory funding objective.

Trustees have two further considerations to bear in mind. Do you want to take social and ethical criteria into account in setting your investment policy? Do you want to exercise your right to vote on company matters? You are formally expected to take and record a decision on both these issues, even if you choose not to become involved. For many smaller schemes, the complications are too great.

Limitations

Although the legal framework encourages you to invest, rather than let the money sit in the bank, there are limitations on the assets that you can consider.

The first point to check is your deed, which might restrict your powers to invest in certain types of asset, and, under the Pensions Act of 2004, you should note that there is a predisposition to holding assets in regulated markets.

Any idea of investing in your employer's business is strictly controlled. No loans and guarantees can be made at all. If an investment is to be made, it must only be on the basis of seeking a return in line with the rest of your assets and the sum cannot exceed 5% of the total value of the scheme.

NOTES

Proper advice

In taking investment decisions, trustees are expected to take 'proper advice'. Failure to comply means that you will be directly answerable to the Financial Services Authority for any mistakes.

For smaller companies, it might mean turning to an independent financial advisor or to your actuary, who is also qualified to give financial advice. Although technically optional, 'investment consultants' are usually necessary on larger schemes to advise you on the asset side of your balance sheet (unlike actuaries who advise on your liabilities).

You delegate day-to-day investment decisions to them and they take on the role of checking whether your funds are being managed effectively, recommending whether you need to switch around any of your holdings. If any mistakes are made, you should not be held personally responsible, as it is the consultants who are regulated by the Financial Services Authority.

Statement of investment principles

However, you do remain responsible for your scheme's investment policy, which governs how any decisions are taken by your investment consultants. At least every three years, you should draw up a 'statement of investment principles' in consultation with your sponsoring employer, although you do not have to agree it with them.

In this you will typically spell out:

- what your objectives for the scheme are;
- how you intend to manage any risks;

- how you intend to allocate investments between different types of asset to meet future liabilities;

- which benchmarks you will use to measure the performance of different types of assets;

- how liquid your assets are and how easily they can be realised;

- how you are performing against the Statutory Funding Objective and how you will take any steps to rectify any shortfalls;

- what weight you give to socially responsible investment;

- and how you will use your voting rights as a shareholder.

In drawing up your statement of investment principles, you are expected to take written advice from an investment consultant and you will need to keep it under review on an ongoing basis. If legislation changes or if there is a significant transaction by your employer, then it is probably going to need to be revised.

BDO Stoy Hayward Investment Management Limited

David Philips

BDO Stoy Hayward Investment Management Limited combines the independent, client-focused approach of a boutique practice with the resources of a major organisation.

The organisation is structured to offer full advice services in the areas of Corporate Pensions and Benefits, Private Client advice and Asset Management and our ability to offer such a complete suite of services makes us fairly unique.

Our proposition is built on the foundations of good quality advice with an unrelenting commitment to client service. With offices throughout the UK and around 200 employees we pride ourselves on our independence and client focused approach. As part of BDO Stoy Hayward LLP, the UK member of BDO International – the world's fifth largest accountancy network – we can boast both strength and depth in our proposition offerings.

The Corporate Pensions and Benefits Team, supported where necessary by our Private Client Team colleagues, advise employers, trustees and individuals on a wide range of areas including:

- Asset allocation modelling and investment planning
- Reviewing existing investment portfolios
- Actuarial services and administration
- Group employee benefits
- Group and stakeholder pension arrangements
- Executive and personal pension counselling
- Pension transfer advice
- Retirement options advice and assistance
- Key man/shareholder protection planning
- Individual protection planning such as life cover and critical illness insurance
- Inheritance tax and estate planning

In the ever-complicated world of pensions we are able to cut through the jargon and regulation to work with you in developing solutions that 'make a positive difference'. Pensions play an ever increasing high profile part in the world of corporate transactions and we have a wealth of experience in guiding businesses through the maze that faces them, and also implementing pension and benefit schemes that help attract, retain and reward employees appropriately.

In the world of Defined Benefit Pensions our actuarial team have amassed a huge working knowledge of dealings with the Pensions Regulator and the Pension Protection Fund. Their experience and support can therefore help you through whatever dealings you have with these bodies and help you understand their role in the regulation of pensions.

Turning to the individual our Private Client Team offer discretionary and advisory services, executive planning and tax mitigation counselling, in the specific areas of Income Tax, Capital Gains Tax and Inheritance Tax. On pensions they also provide specialist advice on Self Invested Personal Pensions (SIPPs), Small Self Administered Schemes (SSASs) and stakeholder pension arrangements for individuals and professional partnerships.

Our Asset Management Team provide asset allocation services, a range of hand-selected investment products as well as comprehensive research and advice on multi-manager investing, hedge funds, property and bonds.

The Asset Management Team have been particularly successful in the discretionary management of pension assets for Defined Benefit Schemes, giving trustees that ability to concentrate their resources into other areas knowing that the scheme assets are being professionally managed to agreed targets and benchmarks. The increased pressures on trustees to have knowledge and control over what can be very complex matters has left many feeling 'overwhelmed' by what regulation now requires of them. At BDO Stoy Hayward Investment Management Limited we pride ourselves on understanding your requirements and providing bespoke solutions that are easy to understand.

For more information please contact:
David Philips, Director
BDO Stoy Hayward Investment Management Ltd
7th & 8th Floors
125 Colmore Row
Birmingham B3 3SD

Tel: 0121 265 7224
Fax: 0121 352 6321
Email: David.philips@bdo.co.uk

Alternatively, visit www.bdo.co.uk to find out more.

BDO Stoy Hayward
Investment Management

Different, honestly.

OK, so that's probably not what you would expect in a pensions ad. But then our advice isn't what you would expect, either. From commodities and active fund management to actuarial, investment management, investment adviser and scheme consultancy – we've built a reputation on a personal approach that is successfully different.

Birmingham
125 Colmore Row,
Birmingham,
B3 3SD
Telephone: 0121 352 6200
david.philips@bdo.co.uk

Bristol
Fourth Floor, 1 Victoria Street,
BS1 6AA
Telephone: 0117 934 2800
david.thompson@bdo.co.uk

Chelmsford
66 Broomfield Road, Chelmsford,
Essex, CM1 1SW
Telephone: 01245 264 644
matthew.phillips@bdo.co.uk

Gatwick
2nd Floor, 2 City Place
Bee Hive Ringroad, Gatwick
West Sussex, RH6 0PA
Telephone: 01293 591000
philip.smithyes@bdo.co.uk

Glasgow
Ballantine House,
168 West George Street,
Glasgow, G2 2 PT
Telephone: 0141 248 3761
alastair.mcquiston@bdo.co.uk

Guildford
Connaught House,
Alexandra Terrace,
Guildford, GU1 3DA
Telephone: 01483 565 666
chris.mascarenhas@bdo.co.uk

Leeds
1 City Square,
Leeds, LS1 2DP
Telephone: 0113 244 3839
adam.wilkinson@bdo.co.uk

London
8 Baker Street,
London, W1U 3LL
Telephone: 020 7486 5888
mark.howlett@bdo.co.uk

Manchester
Commercial Buildings,
11-15 Cross Street,
Manchester M2 1WE
Telephone: 0161 817 3700
phillip.rose@bdo.co.uk

Southampton
Arcadia House, Maritime Walk –
Ocean Village, Southampton
SO14 3TL
Telephone: 023 8088 1700
malcolm.lay@bdo.co.uk

BDO

BDO Stoy Hayward
Investment Management

www.bdo.co.uk

Chapter 4
Asset allocation

As a trustee, you are responsible for setting an investment strategy that is going to secure your members' pensions in the years to come. That does not mean taking a view on whether to buy or sell particular stocks and shares, that is your investment manager's job. But you do have strategic control over the balance of your portfolio. Or, in the case of defined contribution schemes, you can decide what types of investment are on offer to your members.

The balance you choose to strike between different classes of asset and the attitude you take to risk against reward have more far-reaching consequences for the ultimate value of your fund than any individual decisions on whether to buy particular equities, bonds or property.

In allocating your assets, the Pensions Regulator expects you to diversify your holdings and to exercise prudence. In other words, you should not bet the house on anything too risky.

Prudent portfolios

Over the last 60 years, the interpretation of a prudent portfolio has changed dramatically. Originally, only mortgages on real estates and government bonds were considered acceptable. But returns were low and costs were high, so funds moved progressively into equities, commercial property, overseas and derivatives. The risks might have been higher, but so were the rewards. Plus higher returns brought down the costs of running your fund.

By the 1990s, the cult of equity had taken a firm hold. Some pension schemes had allocated up to 90% of their funds to securities traded on public markets such as the London Stock Exchange. The prospect of capital growth plus an annual dividend seemed too good to resist.

These assumptions unwound dramatically in the early 2000s. In two years, the value of equities fell by over 50%. At the same time, a new accounting standard (FRS 17) required listed companies to forecast their future pension liabilities and to reveal their method for calculating them. In an era of low interest rates, this proved painful, because annuities were costing significantly more to buy.

Pension funds found themselves facing ruinously large deficits. Some estimates suggested a national figure as high as £700bn.

New thinking

The shock of these deficits, which was compounded because they had to be declared on company's balance sheets, gave a severe jolt to some hitherto conventional assumptions about how assets should be allocated.

In the bear market of the early 2000s, the risk of relying too heavily on equities was thought by some to be unacceptable. One line of thinking suggested that it would be better to cover your future commitment to pay your members' pensions by buying a portfolio of bonds of equal duration to your liabilities (if you could), so insulating yourself from any falls or rises on financial markets. The trouble was that you would lock yourself into an existing deficit, as the assets would never grow sufficiently to plug any gap.

So, in another challenge to conventional thinking, it has been argued that as a trustee you should tear yourself away from comparing the annual returns on a like-for-like basis with other pension funds and focus on the total return that you are going to have to achieve to meet the liabilities of your particular scheme.

Where you need to make higher returns, then you might consider alternative assets, such as private equity and hedge funds, which are not publicly quoted. Then to guard against economic risks, such as inflation, interest rates and foreign exchange, capital-markets instruments, such as derivatives, might be used.

So the days when trustees could spend a few hours a year making a simplistic split between blue-chip equities, government bonds and commercial property have long gone.

The starting point

The future liabilities of any scheme vary depending on the composition of its membership. Your calculations will depend on whether:

- your members have already retired and are drawing a pension, in which case their priority is certainty of income, so any liability maybe better matched by government bonds.

- your members are still working, so maybe better protected by looking for more long-term growth in the form of equities and property.

- your members have left the organisation to work elsewhere, but have kept their pension rights with you. Again growth assets, such as equities or property, might be best, particularly if there is any risk of inflation.

Year by year, you want to have a clear view of what your cashflow is actually going to be. You can then set a benchmark for a total rate of return to meet your commitments.

Those calculations should include your tolerance for economic risk, notably changes in interest rates, inflation and foreign exchange. You also need to account for the impact for volatility on the stock market and increases in longevity among your members.

However, if you adopt too conservative a stance, your returns may be too low and contributions may have to rise.

Asset classes

Once you have a framework for total return and tolerance of risk in securing your members' pensions, you can take a view on your exposure to the four main asset classes:

1. Equities can be volatile and risky, but offer the potential of higher rewards, particularly in the long-term. They can easily be bought and sold.

2. Bonds are more stable in value, offering a clear stream of income. They are still liquid, but less risk means lower returns.

3. Property is another growth asset, but is usually less volatile than equities. It is harder to liquidate though.

4. Cash is entirely liquid and has minimal risk, but returns are low.

NOTES

Beyond these four main classes, as a trustee you are also likely to consider alternative assets, often holding private equity or hedge funds as satellite holdings, to give yourself the chance of making higher returns, although at more risk.

A portfolio can then be constructed by your investment advisors to plot expected returns against expected risks. By including alternative assets within your holdings, you will have more flexibility in managing your exposure.

Although you will be operating against a long-term benchmark for your rate of return, you have scope to go overweight or underweight on different assets on a tactical basis to take advantage of market fluctuations.

Electronic Governance Solutions

Alastair McLean, UBSi

The pressure on business to improve corporate governance is having a 'knock on' effect with regard to pensions governance. Proposals from the Financial Services Authority requiring listed companies to demonstrate the quality of their internal controls (and the Sarbanes-Oxley Act of 2002 in the USA that affects any entity raising money in the USA) has resulted in pensions governance receiving a higher profile than it has previously.

This higher profile has resulted in the Pension Regulator issuing its Trustee Knowledge and Understanding (TKU) Code of Practice; the requirement that trustees have excellent knowledge and understanding not just of their own scheme, but a good understanding of pensions, funding and investments in general.

To meet the governance standards required, all parties responsible for the pension scheme (be it Chairman, Chief Executive, Finance Director, Human Resource Director, Pensions Manager or Trustee) should be confident that they can answer such questions as:

- Can we be sure that the policies we have put in place have been implemented?
- Are all investment managers following the investment mandates?
- Is the reporting we receive sufficient for us to be comfortable with the way the pension scheme is run?
- Are the Trustees suitably (and demonstrably) skilled and trained to ask appropriate questions of advisors and to make the appropriate decisions concerning investments – or other issues?
- Are our suppliers meeting their service level agreements?
- How easy is it for us to check on the effectiveness of all parties responsible for contributing to the scheme's performance?

Those responsible for the overall governance of the pension scheme need to understand what is expected of them on a personal level and what is expected of their advisers and suppliers. They also need a means of monitoring those activities and the ability to take whatever action is required. This is true whether they represent the trustees' or the employer's interests. This is also true whether the scheme is administered in-house or outsourced to a third party.

The scheme's advisers also need to have a full understanding of the scheme to properly advise the trustees and/or the scheme sponsor.

Electronic Governance Tools

Electronic governance tools (like UBSi's CAGe™) are expected to benefit those with oversight responsibilities for pensions in three main areas:

- Knowledge capture and distribution – including greater empowerment of the scheme sponsors and trustees. CAGe™ can ensure that trustees have access to all the information they need to fulfil their TKU requirements.

- Facilitation of trustee responsibilities through a scheduling and automated alerting system. Tasks considered important can be scheduled, so that timely email reminders are issued to relevant parties. This is particularly beneficial to trustees with 'day jobs' (i.e. other non-pension responsibilities).

- Better and more efficient management of suppliers and advisors.

If, like CAGe™, the governance system also permits collaborative working, this will enable the external scheme advisers to gain a better understanding of the scheme and the issues it faces, which in turn should result in more focused and more relevant advice.

Knowledge Capture

In most organisations pension knowledge is widely distributed. While some knowledge rests with key people such as members of the pensions department, much knowledge rests with third parties (e.g., actuaries, solicitors, investment advisers). This leaves the scheme sponsor and/or Trustees in a potentially vulnerable position.

The 'knowledge capture' benefits of electronic systems include:

- Reduced risks (and implied costs) of 'lost' knowledge – by capturing the existing:

  - historical knowledge; and

  - knowledge of future tasks

  from current advisers and current staff.

- Reduced dependence on third parties who typically hold dispersed knowledge.

- Increased ease and reduced cost of changing third party advisers (or changing team members within an existing third party adviser).

- Centralised documentation ensuring one consistent up-to-date view.

- Reduced cost searching for knowledge and documentation (systems like CAGe™ make even historical paper documentation word searchable).

- Focused information – by creating information 'views' dependent on roles.

- Access to the web-based knowledge allows:
  - home-working
  - non-centralised trustee boards to access all the information they need
  - new trustees to immediately have knowledge at their fingertips.
- Greater trustee empowerment to identify the 'real' issues.
- Increased 'transparency'.

Maintained audit trails.

Governance Benefits

Trustee boards usually consist of people who have 'day jobs' (i.e. other 'non-pension' roles) to perform. A fundamental governance principle is that a trustee should either:

- be assured that required tasks are being performed; OR
- be alerted to the fact that they are not being performed.

A good electronic governance system will be able to issue automated email alerts to trustees (or other profile groups) whenever a task fails to be performed. Under current legislation, it is the trustees who bear the responsibility for these failures and who will be held to account for any 'failures' that occur.

The benefits of a collaborative electronic governance system are:

- Greater ability to demonstrate Trustees are responding to new legislative requirements, such as TKU.
- Reduced risk of exposure to the 'failure' of 'delegates'.
- Clear objective identification of areas where a Trustee is exposed.
- Reassurance that defined tasks have been performed.
- Ability to be notified when certain information is produced.
- Greater empowerment to question 'failed' performance.

Management Benefits

A good electronic system will provide a framework for the management of the pensions function by:

- Automatically chasing statutory and management documents that need to be produced according to timescales, e.g. Trustee papers and minutes.
- Automatically alerting interested parties to the production of a new document.
- Automatically alerting management to the failure of third parties to deliver, in accordance with previously agreed delivery targets.

Thus:

- Management time chasing and distributing information is reduced.
- Supplier responsibilities are clarified.
- Suppliers who 'deliver' (and those who do not) are objectively identified
- There is increased 'transparency' of management activities and supplier performance.

Overall, this reduces the likelihood of non-compliance and associated management risks.

Components of an Electronic Governance System

An electronic governance system should be designed to address the issues outlined earlier. The system will do this by providing one secure location where each of the pension scheme's stakeholders (and advisers) can access and/or provide information in accordance with their position and responsibility. This location can be on the Internet or the Intranet. As pensions governance becomes more complicated with each new piece of legislation and regulation, the system should provide each individual with a personalised view of the documents as well as the communications and analyses necessary for their role. The system should also highlight any that are missing or overdue – at a glance.

The core components of UBSi's CAGe™ system are:

- A summary that provides information about the scheme at a glance.
- A fully searchable document library.
- Modules for Trustee and committee meetings.
- A Trustee compliance module that provides all the information that the Pensions Regulator believes are necessary to undertake that role including:
  - a TKU Checklist with facility to attach training materials; and
  - a TKU Assessment section, which summarises for each trustee their status with regard to their trustee knowledge and understanding.
- 'Adviser' modules.
- An integrated document and task scheduler to assure the trustees that the managers of the scheme are being compliant.

CAGe™ can also be used as a tool to collate and monitor information about:

- Scheme Investments
- Scheme Liabilities
- Scheme Stewardship.

Within the new pensions environment, all trustees need to be aware of their oversight responsibilities and be given the tools and information to do this. Electronic governance tools (like CAGe™) can meet those needs.

Part

2

Core assets

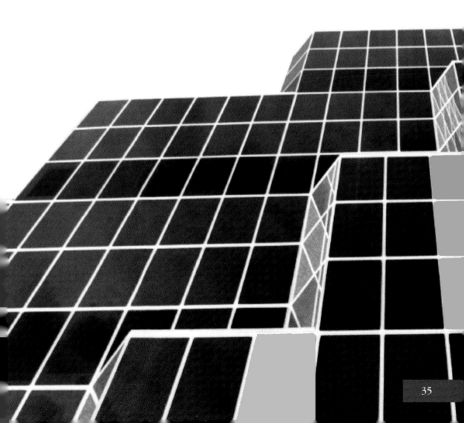

Chapter 5

Quoted equities (shares)

When you buy shares in a company listed on a stock exchange ('quoted'), you are becoming one of its shareholders with a claim on its future profits which will be paid to you twice a year in the form of a dividend. Alongside this regular stream of income, the value of your investment can appreciate.

Your shares make you a part-owner with voting rights, so you have some influence over how a company is managed. However, you rank behind other creditors in the event of any failure or closure, which is why equities command a 'risk premium' over other assets.

Equities have traditionally formed the core of most pension funds, accounting nowadays for 64% of all investments. The attraction is that historically they have proved to be the most attractive asset class. In the UK in the last ten years, the total returns from divided payments and capital gains have together averaged 7.9% p.a.

But as highly liquid investments traded daily on stock exchanges, the value of equities can rise or fall and dramatically. In 2002, returns fell by 22.7%, and rose by 16.8% in 2006.

As well as falling and rising capital values, the payment of dividends can also be unpredictable, particularly in smaller growth companies who are looking to re-invest their profits.

Such volatility can makes shares unsuitable for covering liabilities in the short-term, particularly if employers are underwriting pensions in a defined benefit scheme. But, in the longer term, the upside for members can be significant. In defined contribution schemes, where investment risk falls on individual employees, they may well be attracted by the prospect of higher returns.

Future returns

Profits fluctuate both in individual companies and in economies as a whole, so projecting values into the future cannot be made with great certainty. However, to calculate the funding requirements for pension schemes, some view of a share's relative attractiveness has to be reached.

Price/earnings (PE) ratios and dividend yields (DY) are two common methods. In a PE ratio, you divide the company's current share price by the earnings per share. A low figure, such as 8, suggests a well-established company with a steady stream of revenue, where investors have low expectations for significant growth. Conversely, a high figure, such as 20, reveals a willingness to pay a premium for higher future earnings.

The DY is a ratio between the annual dividend and the current share price. For investors in search of high yields, who want to protect themselves against any cuts in income, it is also worth checking to see whether the proportion of profits that is being paid to shareholders can be realistically maintained.

Growth or value

Shares are often characterised as growth or value investments. Growth stocks, such as technology companies operating in new markets, typically have a high PE ratio and a low DY, because they are thought to hold out the prospect of higher earnings in future.

Companies in mature markets with a low PE ratio and a high DY, such as utilities, are described as value stocks. They offer stable earnings but have limited scope for dramatic future growth. Spotting such companies that are being undervalued by the market has proved to be a highly successful strategy for some investors.

Large cap or small cap

In the last 50 years, smaller listed companies in the UK have out-performed the market as a whole, although their performance against large companies fluctuates over time. During the 1990s, small caps were 8% behind the rest of the market, but in the last three years they have been 10% ahead.

Performance measures

To measure investment performance against a benchmark for the market, a large number of indices have been developed. In the UK, the FTSE 100 brings together the top 100 companies listed on the London Stock Exchange. Each constituent is weighted according to its value to give an average which is then quoted as a single figure.

The FTSE 250 comprises the next largest companies and the FTSE 350 combines the top 100 and 250. The FTSE Small

Cap consists of any company outside the top 350 and the FTSE All Share brings all these indices together.

In the US, the S&P 500 is the leading index that measures the average value of the top 500 listed companies. In Germany it is the DAX; in Japan it's the Nikkei 225 and in France, the CAC 40. MSCI Global is a worldwide index and the Dow Jones Stoxx 600 covers Europe.

As well as being able to follow each main equity market, you can also use specialist indices to see how different sectors are performing, which allows you to compare how UK companies are performing against their global counterparts.

International switch

In the UK, there has been a decisive shift among pension funds in the last decade towards international equities. According to UBS, a global asset manager, the weighting given to UK and international shares reached parity for the first time last year. Each now account for 32% of assets invested by pension funds.

London remains an attractive destination for funds because it lists so many internationally focused companies who pay their dividends in sterling, which eliminates any currency risk if that is how your liabilities are paid.

But you might want to diversify your risk away from the UK and gain exposure to other growth markets, such as technology, that are less well represented on the FTSE 100, which is dominated by banks, telecoms and oil.

You might also consider investing in emerging markets, where there is scope for aggressive growth. Because the level of country risk is much higher than in the US or

NOTES

Europe, you can make spectacular gains if your timing is right. In 2006, the Chinese stock market rose by over 90% and in 2005 Egypt was up by over 150%.

But these are new markets for shares, so the risks of a sharp correction are equally high. In 2006, Saudi Arabia was down by nearly 50% and then in the wake of a currency crisis in 1998 the Russian market fell by almost 90%.

Passive or active

To gain access to such growth opportunities without losing your shirt, you have to work with a firm of fund managers. As a trustee, you will delegate investment decisions to them, so you have to choose them on the basis of their experience and expertise, as well as on the strength of their investment process and their team.

You have to be convinced that they can use these qualities to make an 'active' choice of shares in line with your statement of investment principles that is going to outperform the market as a whole, not just next year but on a consistent basis.

These superior returns should be made after accounting the fund manager's costs, which are typically 1%. If ignored and allowed to compound on an annual basis, these charges can significantly harm your eventual returns.

The alternative, as for 30% of pension funds invested in equities, is to track one of the main indices passively, such as the FTSE 100 or the FTSE All Share. At a typical rate of 0.1%, the costs are lower and you reduce some of the risk attached to investment decisions. Your funds automatically replicate the make-up of the market.

The drawback is that even in the FSTE Allshare, the value of your shares will be heavily concentrated in the top dozen global corporations, which undermines the virtue for taking a diversified approach.

There is no definitive conclusion whether you should invest actively or passively. For core holdings to cover short-term liabilities, it may make sense to hold a UK index passively, while taking a more aggressive approach for longer term liabilities.

Investment styles

For fund managers, the onus is on adopting investment styles that are going to produce superior returns. Typically they will assume a growth or value approach. They will also tend to take a top-down or bottom-up view.

Top-down managers look first at overall economic perform-ance, as well as social trends, to determine which assets and sectors are likely to do well in the next cycle of activity. Once an area of potential has been identified, a close analysis is made of financial statements to uncover any risks. Bottom-up relies on picking individual shares that are going to beat the market in the short-term.

Managers then typically run a selection of funds that specialise by:

- geographical territory, such as the US or emerging markets
- sectors, such as global life sciences or global leisure
- size of company, such as global corporations or small caps

They might also 'tilt' their portfolio towards specific events or themes. Which companies might benefit from a rise in commodity prices? Who is highly exposed in a particular market? And who displays a particular set of financial characteristics?

Held to account

As well as ensuring fund managers stick to your statement of investment principles, trustees want to ensure that their funds do not perform any worse than average.

Benchmarks, either in the form of indices or rankings, become important in judging how fund managers are performing against their peer group.

To prevent fund managers investing too heavily in any one particular share, many trustees ask them to invest on a 'constrained' basis. They are given an index as a basis, but they are allowed to use their discretion to go underweight or overweight on one particular stock.

While this approach removes the risk of doing significantly worse than the market, it also caps the degree to which funds can do any better. As a result, increasing numbers of trustees are decoupling performance from traditional investment benchmarks and allowing fund managers more room and flexibility to invest on an 'unconstrained' basis.

Active Liability Driven Investing

Henderson liability driven solutions

- **Economies of scale**
  - Over a £1bn managed in active liability driven solutions on behalf of UK pension funds
  - Over £6bn managed in total liability benchmarked portfolios with various performance targets

- **Experience in liability hedging**
  - Over 25 years experience of innovation in liability matching programs
  - A leading counterparty in interest rate, inflation and credit default swaps market

- **Ability to generate absolute returns**
  - Strong active management track records in broad range of return sources within and beyond fixed income
  - Mixture of clients using leveraged and un-leveraged solutions with objectives ranging from LIBOR +50bps to LIBOR +400bps over bespoke benchmarks

- **Flexibility & client focus through segregated accounts**
  - Bespoke solutions tailored to clients' desired level of precision, cost, benchmark selection, performance targets and governance giving greater flexibility than pooled solutions

- **Business commitment**
  - 9 specialists supported by fixed income team of over 50 investment professionals contribute to liability driven mandates
  - Significant IT investment gives Henderson the operational platform to manage, control and report derivative exposure for clients

- **Risk management**
  - Use of leading edge tools combined with a common sense approach to risk management

Return seeking capabilities (Diversified Fixed Income)

Diversification by asset class, strategy and time

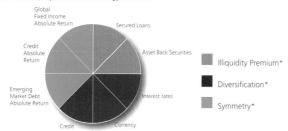

* A number of these asset classes will have shared characteristics representing more than 100 uncorrelated strategies

www.henderson.com/institutional

For further information, please contact Andrew Fraser, Director of Institutional Business:

email: andrew.fraser@henderson.com

Telephone: + 44 (0)20 7818 3388

Source: Henderson Global Investors, as at 31 August 2007.

Liability driven investing – thinking beyond the benchmark to generate fixed income returns

Andrew Fraser, Director of Institutional Business at Henderson Global Investors, considers the options available to fixed income investors aiming to move beyond the boundaries of traditional bond portfolio mandates.

Liability Driven Investment (LDI) has led to a realignment of pension fund objectives, giving trustees the option of moving away from benchmark-hugging portfolios and making the liability itself the benchmark with which to measure performance. For institutional investors, fixed income portfolios with their consistent and steady returns have traditionally been the logical choice when looking for liability driven investment vehicles. But the positive factors that can help to push bond fund returns upwards when equities are performing poorly can also have the opposite effect at different times in the market cycle. The dilemma facing institutional investors is how to obtain long-term positive returns that match their liability-driven requirements, without exposing their investments to substantially greater risk.

Portfolio diversity is vital

We believe that LDI is not a product, but a framework for managing assets to maximise returns while minimising risk relative to the estimated liabilities. The key to meeting this challenge lies in active portfolio management that ensures diversity across all fixed income asset classes. Bond market prices ultimately reflect their underlying fundamental values. However, at any point in time bond prices may differ significantly from their fair value estimate. These deviations result in various opportunities to add value over the market cycle in many different areas of the bond and currency markets.

By widening the investment field to include currencies and secured loans, managers can also hedge away unwanted exposures. Derivatives can be used by managers to reduce risk, use leverage to increase weighting within an area where they have the most conviction, and to generate returns that are uncorrelated to equity or bond markets. The use of 'long/short' – one of the most popular hedge fund strategies – is also helping so-called 'traditional' bond portfolio managers to deliver enhanced returns without the need to increase risk and overall volatility.

Are hedge fund capabilities suitable for bond portfolios?

One frequent concern among institutional investors is that while permitting hedging (or shorting) in a portfolio gives fund managers more scope to generate returns, it also increases the scope for fund managers to lose money. The value of a long position in an equity can only fall by 100% (if the stock becomes literally worthless). However, the holder of a short position makes money if the stock *falls in value*. If the value of the stock rises instead of falls, potential losses are uncapped, as there is theoretically no limit as to how far a stock could rise. The exact opposite is true in the case of fixed income. The price of a bond is unlikely to rise much above 100, offering little reward for a long investor. However, the price can fall all the way to zero on default, offering a significant opportunity for the holder of a short position in the bond. Shorting techniques will be most successfully applied by fund managers who already have extensive short-selling experience and relevant risk controls, where it already forms an integral part of their investment process.

Innovation is not for everyone

This kind of portfolio freedom may not be to everyone's taste. Just as different clients have to consider their individual attitudes towards risk, fund managers have to think about whether they have the expertise, appetite and technical support needed to use these wider powers to their full potential. Managers also need to feel confident that they have a back-office infrastructure capable of handling the complex fund management techniques and risk measurement calculations required. Therefore, it seems that the larger asset management companies with greater experience in liability-driven investment vehicles and a proven track record of using hedge fund techniques will have a first mover advantage when it comes to implementing these skills within 'traditional' portfolios.

Meeting the needs of LDI

No longer are bond fund managers driven by a herd mentality – their ability to go further to find good investment opportunities can now be properly rewarded. They can adopt a more aggressive stance if they believe the market is working in their favour or, perhaps more importantly, they can hedge their positions and take a more defensive position if required.

Through the use of leverage and greater diversification across a number of non-correlated alpha sources, fixed income fund managers can enhance performance and generate hedge fund-type returns for LDI-focused investors and, more importantly, breathe new life into an asset class such as fixed income.

Henderson Global Investors manages over £1 billion in active liability driven investments on behalf of UK pension funds, and has over 25 years' experience of innovation in liability matching programs.

Fixed income portfolios – steps to success

- Identifying the maximum number of uncorrelated return opportunities.
- Pragmatic investment approach driven by absolute return mentality.
- Exploiting longer term themes whilst harnessing short-term volatility.
- Experience in asset allocation and rigorous stock selection.
- Strong derivative capabilities.
- Risk management embedded in the investment process.

For more information please contact:
Tel: +44 (0)20 7818 5050

Alternatively, visit www.henderson.com/institutional to find out more.

Chapter 6

Bonds

When you buy a bond, you are lending money to a government or a corporation. In return, you will be paid a fixed rate of interest, a 'coupon', at regular intervals before your original investment, the 'principal', is redeemed on a set date.

As a trustee, bonds offer you a predictable stream of funding, which can be structured to give a close cashflow match for future liabilities. In particular, it gives you the opportunity to construct a 'safe harbour' as a low-risk core to your holdings.

But, over time, expectations change. When bonds are issued, the coupon is set at a rate high enough above the prevailing interest on bank deposits to attract you as an investor. This margin can be easily eroded by moves in interest rates or inflation. So, in managing a portfolio, you will want to think about buying and selling bonds, as a way of making sure that you continue to gain the best rates of return.

Fixed income

Often known as 'fixed income securities', bonds are usually issued by organisations for funding over extended periods of up to 30 years. In the case of government bonds, or 'gilts' as they are called in the UK, the returns are guaranteed.Their relative lack of volatility means that you are unlikely to make any significant capital gains.

For corporate bonds, the risks are greater either in the form of a default on payment or, more probably, a credit downgrade. However, the potential returns are higher, particularly in the case of 'junk' bonds, which are those without an investment rating.

Forty years ago, pension funds typically allocated half their assets to bonds. By the mid 1990s, this figure had fallen to 10%, but since then it steadily rose to reach 24% in 2006.

Within the fixed-income universe, there are many different categories of bond, which have different profiles of risk and return. They are also highly liquid, so can easily be bought and sold, allowing your asset managers to fine-tune the match against the liabilities of your fund. At the end of 2006, according to Merrill Lynch, the size of the UK market was $929bn for government bonds and $564bn for non-government bonds.

Globally, the size of bond markets has doubled in the last ten years. This growth has been led by non-government debt, as more prudent fiscal policies are pursued in the developed economies.

For those looking for higher returns on government bonds, emerging markets have become a significant asset class in their own right. Since 1991, according to JP Morgan, they have shown an annual return of 15.3%, despite sharp falls in 1994 (-18.3%) and in 1998 (-11.5%). Over 50 governments in the developing world now issue bonds in major currencies, such as the dollar and the euro, and 25 raise money in their local currency as well.

Other types of bonds

Beyond the basic formula of principal, coupon and maturity, there are multiple types of bonds:

- Index linked: both the coupon and the principal are adjusted to changes in inflation. Pioneered by the UK government in the 1980s, these bonds can be particularly attractive to pension funds, as their liabilities are inflation proofed.

- Eurobonds: securities that are issued internationally in leading currencies (not necessarily the euro), which usually have a fixed coupon.

- Zero coupons: these bonds only make a single payment on maturity and pay no interest, so are generally issued at deep discount to the original value (par).

- Floating rate: coupons are linked to the bank rate, so payments vary.

- Convertibles: these give you an option to turn bonds into equity at a later date.

- Calls and puts: for a premium, an issuer can redeem (or call) a bond prior to maturity. A put option gives the investor the power to ask for early redemption, usually in return for lower coupons.

- Junk bonds: these are high-yield bonds with a sub-investment rating, which offer higher returns but at more risk.

- STRIPS (Separate Trading of Registered Interest and Principal of Securities): these bonds allow the coupon and the principal to be traded separately.

- Asset-backed: these are often used for mortgages, where an underlying asset secures the bond's cash flow.

The terms for particular bond issues are often open for negotiation, so investors can protect themselves against specific risks. So a corporate may have to agree not to issue any more debt or dispose of any of its assets.

Yields and price

The most common measure for valuing a bond is the 'gross redemption yield,' which expresses the combined return of holding it all the way to maturity and re-investing the coupons. It gives you a percentage that represents the compounded annual return that you can expect.

Over time, the yields that you expect as an investor can change significantly either because of economic fundamentals, particularly interest rates and inflation, or because of variations in the credit quality of a particular bond.

But, by definition, the income from bonds is fixed. So if investors require a higher yield, then the price of the bond will have to fall. The coupon can then represent a higher proportion of the price.

In other words, yields have an inverse relationship with the price of a bond. When yields are rising, prices fall. Similarly, if yields are falling, prices will rise: the fixed income becomes a lower proportion of price, reflecting the lower returns expected by investors.

When yields are already high, the impact of any changes is relatively low. But when low interest rates apply, prices become more volatile. 'Duration' is a technical term for

NOTES

establishing the price sensitivity of a bond. Generally, the longer the term, the higher a bond's duration, making it more sensitive to changes in yield. It is a useful measure in re-allocating portfolios, particularly as prices tend to increase more quickly when yields fall, then they decrease when yields rise.

The yield curve

Usually, long-dated bonds have a higher yield, which reflects investors' concerns about risks over a period of 20, 30 or even 50 years. Because payments fall so far into the future, the trading of these bonds tends to be more volatile than short-dated ones.

So, in plotting yields against the term of the bond, the line usually curves upwards over the years. In normal circumstances, you might expect to see a difference of between 1% between short-dated and long-dated bonds.

In practice, investors' expectations about economic risks can cause the curve to flatten in later years, particularly if they think interest rates are too high in the short-term. In addition, the rules of supply and demand continue to apply.

Governments have been following more prudent fiscal policies, while at the same time pension funds have been seeking to use bonds to match their future liabilities. As a result in the UK over the last two years, the yield curve has flattened to the point where rates are higher in the short-term, creating an 'inverse' yield curve.

Economic risks

The two principal risks for any fixed income security are interest rates and inflation. Any change in interest rates has a direct impact on yields and prices, although bonds have differing levels of sensitivity, and inflation erodes the value of both the coupons and the principal.

If investors buy international bonds, they open themselves up to the further risk of movement in exchange rates. In addition, other countries are usually at different points in the economic cycle, so the assumptions underpinning long-term interest rates will not be the same. So, a high yield may actually not represent good value, unless the risks are properly understood.

Credit risks

In addition to these economic variations, coporate bonds carry an extra layer of risk, as they are more likely to experience difficulties with their payments or, in the worst case, become insolvent.

Rating agencies, such as Moody's and Standard & Poor's, take a view on the potential for any loss. For governments, such as the UK and the US, with excellent credit quality, they will give a rating of AAA, which falls all the way down to D for less reliable organisations.

For bonds on lower ratings, investors expect more interest over a risk-free gilt. An extra 1% – 1.5% on a relatively secure A-rated corporate may well be attractive for a pension fund, particularly if they hold a portfolio of such bonds.

NOTES

54

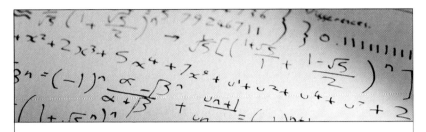

Property investment – an essential core for pension fund investment portfolios

Charles Follows, Director, Head of UK Research & Strategy, ING Real Estate Investment Management

The average pension fund holds about 7.6% of its portfolio in property (*The WM Company, Q2 2007*). That implies that the other 82.4% of pension funds have not been invested in the top performing asset class of the last 1, 5, 10 and 20 years (to 31 December 2006, *source: IPD UK Annual digest*). Why is this? Is this property aversion a risky strategy for the typical pension fund trustee? At ING Real Estate Investment Management (ING REIM) we believe that such a low property weighting is undesirable and risky. Property's portfolio attributes are such that it overcomes many of the undeniable challenges to successful property investment.

The structure of a pension fund portfolio will reflect its specific objectives and maturity, and a sensibly structured and managed property investment portfolio is an essential part of the core investment portfolio for the prudent pension fund. The UK's stock of investment grade commercial property is about 12% of the potential total investment universe of the UK, across equities, bonds and property. Therefore, a market neutral investment portfolio should have a property weight of above 10%.

The chart below shows how property has produced excellent absolute returns and risk adjusted returns since 1980.

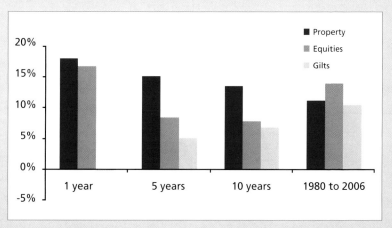

Asset Class Total Returns Annualised

Source: IPD UK Annual Digest

1980 to 2006			
	Property	**Equities**	**Gilts**
Annualised Total Return	11.2%	14.0%	10.5%
Standard Deviation	8.3%	15.2%	11.6%
Risk/Return Ratio	1.413	1.043	0.982

Risk and return
Source: IPD UK Annual Digest, Bank of England, ING REIM

In the long-term it is reasonable to expect property returns to lie between equity returns and bonds returns. Property is a hybrid investment with equity like capital growth returns on top of a solid secure bond like stable income return. The property income return, at 4.9% pa in July 2007 (*source: IPD UK Monthly Digest*) is secured by a lease with an average unexpired length of 12.3 years (full lease terms on all leases, weighted by rent passing (*source BPF /IPD Annual Lease review*). Since 1980 about 60% of the total return from property has been delivered by this stable and secure income. Even in the depths of the early 1990s economic recession the typical property investment portfolio continued to deliver income growth, whilst many equity companies passed or cut dividends.

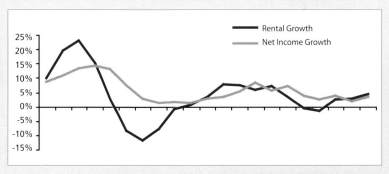

Rental v Property Income Growth
Source: IPD UK Annual Digest

In addition to excellent absolute and risk adjusted returns, property adds very valuable diversification to a multi-asset portfolio. The table below shows the long-term correlations of returns since 1980 for the three principal asset classes and cash. A low level of property correlation is evident and by blending a suitable property portfolio into a multi-asset class portfolio, the prudent investor can reduce risk and volatility without unduly diminishing returns.

1980 to 2006				
	Property	**Equities**	**Gilts**	**Cash**
Property	1.00	0.18	-0.10	-0.04
Equities	0.18	1.00	0.36	0.31
Gilts	-0.10	0.36	1.00	0.12
Cash	-0.04	0.31	0.12	1.00

Total Return Correlations over the last 27 years

Source: IPD UK Annual Digest, ING REIM

Nevertheless optimisation analysis always suggests unrealistically high property weightings. With an LDI approach, the security of the property income stream fits well with pension fund liabilities. Both approaches give property a central place in a diversified and risk managed portfolio.

Property, like all asset classes, requires specialist and rigorous research led management. At ING REIM, we structure our clients' portfolios to ride market cycles with ING efficient portfolios tuned for upswings and downturns. We use our research and forecasting to make tactical allocation switches and to ensure the best stock selection.

The challenges with property investment include its heterogeneous nature, large lumpy lot sizes and potential illiquidity. These can be addressed by structuring a portfolio with a blend of directly owned property, indirect vehicles, and public listed securities, REITS, property derivatives and structured products. The property market offers a range of investment opportunities both in the UK and across global markets. By blending these different options, market segments and geographies, a unique portfolio is assembled to meet specific return objectives and risk tolerance. For most investors, their bond and cash holdings provide the portfolio liquidity.

Property should be a central part of the core portfolio of the prudent pension fund, to give it access to healthy absolute returns and very attractive risk adjusted returns.

For more information please contact Peter Macpherson:

Tel: +44 (0)20 7767 5505
Email: peter.macpherson@ingrealestate.co.uk

Alternatively, visit www.ingrealestate.com to find out more.

REAL ESTATE INVESTMENT MANAGEMENT

Cultivating growth
building value

Since 1980, ING Real Estate Investment Management has grown to become one of the UK's leading property investment managers. Today, the company has over GBP 8 billion of assets under management and a distinguished reputation for success.

We offer our services to every class of investor – retail and institutional, local authority and corporate, UK and international.
Those services include:

> Direct Investments

> Listed & Unlisted Pooled Funds

> Multi-Manager & Fund of Funds

For further information, please contact:
Peter Macpherson
T +44 (0) 20 7767 5505
E peter.macpherson@ingrealestate.co.uk

ING Real Estate Investment Management
6th Floor, 60 London Wall,
London, EC2M 5TQ

Services relating to direct property are provided by ING Real Estate Investment Management (UK) Limited. All services that are regulated by the Financial Services Authority ("FSA") are provided by ING Real Estate Investment Management (UK Funds) Limited which is authorised and regulated by the FSA.

REAL ESTATE

ING

UK property investors looking overseas

Chris Saunders, Director and Head of Investment
Strategy, DTZ Investment Management

The UK property market looks to be nearing the end of a yield cycle that has
rewarded investors with very strong returns. Going forward UK returns are
likely to be much lower and investors are starting to look elsewhere. Over
the past year an ever-increasing number of UK institutional property
investors have been looking to invest in continental Europe.

UK Investment in Continental Europe

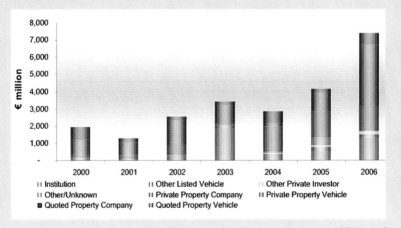

Source: DTZ Research

Investing across Europe provides access to a much larger investible Universe.
Although it may be the largest individual property market within Europe,
DTZ Research estimates that the UK makes up just 15% of total European
commercial property stock, which is considered to be in the region of
€3.9trillion. Accessing European markets, therefore, opens up a range of
additional investment opportunities, even for UK-domiciled investors that
have traditionally benefited from a large, transparent and liquid domestic
property market.

A UK portfolio investing across the different property types provides
limited diversification, with returns across the three major sectors, office,
retail and industrial highly correlated. All the sectors are driven by the
same economic and property market cycle. The European property market
provides exposure to a number of economies and property markets that
are not all moving at the exact same pace or in the same direction. Of most
significance is that most have property market cycles that are not aligned
with the UK, thereby providing diversification benefits to the UK investor.

The variance in property market cycles across Europe also means that there is greater diversity in expected returns. We expect little difference between UK property sector returns over the next five years. In contrast, the variance in our forecasts for the European property market is greater. This provides greater opportunities for the more selective of investors to earn superior returns.

One reason for the differences in expected returns across Europe is that it consists of both mature and emerging property markets. There is an opportunity to capture the benefits of improving transparency and investor interest in emerging markets, especially those in Central and Eastern Europe. Likewise, there are a number of emerging property formats on the continent, such as modern shopping centres and retail warehousing, that provide excellent investment opportunities.

Like the UK, continental Europe has also seen fairly strong returns in recent years on the back of falling yields. However, in our view, Europe is lagging behind the UK property cycle and there remains scope for further yield compression. Crucially the gap between property yields and borrowing costs remains positive, whereas in the UK this is no longer true. The Eurozone economy, which has been subdued over recent years, is also showing signs of improving with an upturn in domestic demand. A stronger economy should translate into better rental growth prospects.

For those investors looking to invest large sums into European property direct investment remains an option. We estimate that in order to achieve a diversified exposure across Europe through direct ownership a portfolio size of at least €300 million would be required. This is a considerable amount of investment, and represents far more than the average UK institutional investor is looking to allocate to the region. In order to build and manage a direct portfolio effectively you need to have access to a network of real estate professionals on the ground in continental Europe. Direct investment, therefore, only makes sense for the larger investors, who are able to capture the economies of scale.

An alternative way of investing in European property is through unlisted pooled property funds. These funds provide a property style return without the complexities and scale required for direct investment. By pooling investments together pooled investment funds provide more diversified exposure to assets than could be achieved by investing the equivalent capital directly in property.

A number of Pan-European balanced funds exist that can provide a broad exposure across sectors and regions, which effectively enable an investor to 'buy Europe'. In our view investing via a balanced fund does have its drawbacks. Europe is also a fairly big market, and it is difficult for a single balanced fund manager to be an expert in every region and sector.

At DTZ Investment Management we favour investing with specialist fund managers that have a specific focus on a particular sector or geography. By investing with the 'best' manager within each market we believe you are able to maximise the benefits of management expertise. However, high minimum investment holdings mean that investment of €50million plus is required in order to build a diversified portfolio within a segregated account.

However, one way smaller investors can achieve access to a specialist fund approach is to invest via a fund of funds product. A fund of funds manager can provide the necessary expertise to select and manage a portfolio of specialist investments, and the pooled nature of the vehicle means it is accessible for smaller investors. Investing in a fund that consists of series of underlying funds provides an extra layer of diversification for investors. The drawback of this approach is the additional layer of fees the investor incurs, but in our opinion the potential performance benefits of a selective approach outweigh the costs.

Weaker prospects at home, and the potential for further yield shift in European markets suggest that now is a good time to invest. Advances in the investment products now available also make accessing the market easier than ever for foreign investors.

For more information please contact:

Tel: +44 (0)20 7643 6399
Email: chris.saunders@dtz.com

Alternatively, visit www.dtz.co.uk to find out more.

Chapter 7
Property

In allocating assets, property holds a distinctive appeal for pension trustees. It combines a more predictable stream of income than equities with more scope for making capital gains than bonds. It also performs independently of either of them, making it a good way for trustees to diversify the risks in their scheme.

Returns

Pension schemes usually invest directly into commercial property, such as offices, shops and business parks, or indirectly into shares or funds. Returns are measured by adding income from rents to capital gains in the form of rising property prices.

Over the last 30 years, investors have on average made 12.7% a year, which is below equities at 15.4%, but these earnings have been much less volatile. The last losses in property happened in the downturn of the early 1990s and even then they were relatively minor.

This steadiness, which has encouraged some investors to put property in the same bracket as bonds, has a twofold explanation. Unlike equities where the level of dividends is at the discretion of a company's directors, rent is secured by contract and must be paid. Tenants are normally on leases of around 15 years and notice must be given of a vacancy. If any breach in the terms occurs, deposits are held as protection.

On the capital side, property is closely linked to the current performance of the economy, rather than to how financial markets expect it will perform in the future. As a result, it is less volatile than equities with fewer peaks and troughs in value. It also has an inbuilt protection against inflation as rents and property prices will automatically adjust during negotiations with occupants.

Because of these structural differences in property as an asset, it has a low level of sensitivity to changes in the value of equities and bonds, which makes it an effective way of diversifying the risk in any portfolio. Currently 7% of assets within pension schemes are allocated to property, which represents a gentle rise over the last ten years.

Capital intensive

Unlike equities and bonds, there is no central exchange for property and no standard investment vehicle. Assets are illiquid. They have to be individually valued and bought or sold in large units.

The costs of making a transaction are high, notably in the form of fees for professional advice and stamp duty. Each property then has to be directly maintained and managed. For smaller investors, it may prove too capital intensive to own property directly, although there are a number of ways of gaining exposure indirectly.

In the last ten years, the market in the UK has become more competitive. Easier credit terms have encouraged more investors and developers to pursue projects. As a result, many pension schemes have started to give more serious consideration to international projects.

Direct or indirect

In a direct investment, investors acquire the freehold of a property, giving them the power as landlord to improve it for potential occupants. Or, if they are in partnership with a developer and a construction company, they might take a long lease.

Although some pension schemes have started to diversify into leisure centres and hotels, they tend to concentrate on one of three areas:

1. Offices, particularly in London, where returns depend on timing. Investment-grade offices have historically been the most cyclical part of the property market, although a repeat of a crash on the late 1980s/early 1990s seems unlikely.

2. Retail, which has been a consistently strong performer for pension funds in the last decade, based on the strength of consumer spending in the UK.

3. Industrial, which now tends to mean business parks or distribution centres rather than factories. Until two years ago, it had a consistent record for giving the best returns in the sector.

Despite the interest of individual investors in buy-to-let properties, pension funds have generally not become involved in residential property because the capital sums are too low to justify the costs in making a transaction and maintaining each property.

As an investor if you wish to gain exposure to property without incurring the high upfront costs of making a direct purchase, there are a number of indirect options:

- You can invest in individually quoted property shares or in a tracker fund linked to the property index. The trouble is that returns are often affected as much by wider trends on the equity markets as by what is happening in property.

- You can join other pension schemes in a pooled fund that aims to invest directly in a number of diverse commercial properties on your behalf.

- You could subscribe to a PUT (Property Unit Trust), which are schemes that specialise in holding property assets. As an investor, you hold units in the portfolios as a whole. Shares are not traded on the open market. Instead the manager of the trust quotes a daily price at which units can be bought and sold.

- Since January 2007, REITs (Real Estate Investment Trusts) have been available in the UK. They are vehicles that allow for transparent tax. In the US, they have proved to be a highly effective proxy for holding property directly.

- If you are a larger investor you might consider a limited property partnership, which is usually a privately held offshore fund that aims to borrow money to secure higher returns on its properties.

Local or international

Property is so subject to particular conditions and laws within each country that historically investments have only been made locally. However, the strength of property markets and interest in new projects is stimulating awareness in other markets in America, Europe and Asia.

At the same time, the terms on which leases are granted are starting to show signs of convergence. Terms of between 5 and 15 years are common coupled with regular rent reviews.

Compared to equities and bonds, there has also been a lack of comparable data against which to benchmark investment decisions. However, intensive efforts are being made to improve transparency by standardising techniques for valuation and for measuring performance.

Although risks remain, particularly in foreign exchange and in planning, property is moving towards establishing itself as an asset that can be managed on a global basis.

PITMANS and PITMANS TRUSTEES LIMITED

Pitmans is a leading specialist commercial law firm and offers a comprehensive legal service to a broad range of national and international clients. It has a substantial pensions department comprised of sixteen experts which is the largest in the South East outside London.

The pensions department offers a full range of pensions related legal services, and its lawyers advise trustees and employers on all aspects of occupational and personal pension schemes. The department also offers an independent trustee service in the form of *Pitmans Trustees Limited*, a wholly owned subsidiary of Pitmans.

Pitmans' practice areas

Pitmans' main pensions practice areas are as follows:

Pensions advice

The advent of the Pensions Act 2004 and the tax simplification changes implemented with effect from 6 April 2006, have resulted in trustees and employers needing to take specialist advice on the new legislation. Pitmans regularly advises on all compliance issues, together with matters relating to trustees' duties, restructuring, scheme wind-ups and mergers, benefit design and conversion from final salary to money purchase.

Pensions documentation

The pensions team drafts the full range of pension scheme documentation in plain English in a user-friendly manner. The Pensions Act 2004 and tax changes mean that all schemes need to review and amend their governing rules, and the team can produce new deeds to reflect the legislative requirements.

Mergers and acquisitions

Pensions can be a key element in corporate transactions. Pitmans has considerable expertise in assisting with 'clearance' applications and negotiating with the Pensions Regulator in the context of a wide variety of transactions.

Investment and funding

The new funding regime introduced by the Pensions Act 2004 means that final salary scheme trustees and employers must comply with complex legal requirements. Pitmans has extensive experience of clarifying and advising on the new regime, and works closely with actuaries and fund managers.

Pitmans Trustees Limited ('PTL')

PTL accepts appointments both to ongoing schemes and schemes that are winding-up, and acts as an independent trustee in relation to all kinds of pension schemes. PTL is on the Pensions Regulator's register of approved independent trustees and can act as sole trustee or jointly with other trustees.

Appointing PTL can add value to a pension scheme in many ways, in particular:

- the presence of an independent trustee can reassure the other trustees that the trustee board as a whole can demonstrate the new statutory standard of knowledge and understanding of legal, investment and funding issues relating to pension schemes required by the Pensions Act 2004;

- PTL can be particularly helpful in assisting in managing conflicts of interest – for example in relation to funding matters, or if the employer wants to close the scheme, and the existing trustees are also directors of the employer;

- trustee training: PTL can provide training to trustees regarding their duties and responsibilities;

- members will feel more confident with a professional trustee on the board, as PTL's role is to act in the members' best interests.

Why appoint Pitmans or PTL?

The advantages of appointing Pitmans pensions team to provide legal advice or PTL to act as independent trustee include:

- an informed and professional team;

- a personal service;

- a competitive fee structure which reflects our location and size;

- a swift and timely service: service standards and deadlines are agreed and met;

- a proactive approach: developments are raised as and when they happen.

For more information please contact:

David Archer – Pitmans Partner and Director of PTL
Direct Line Tel: 0118 957 0303
Email: darcher@pitmans.com

David Hosford – Pitmans Partner and Director of PTL
Direct Line Tel: 0118 957 0363
Email: dhosford@pitmans.com

Andrew Gaspar – Director of PTL
Direct Line Tel: 0118 957 0320
Email: agaspar@pitmans.com

www.pitmans.com
www.pitmanstrustees.com

Independent Trustee of the Year, 2006

Chapter 8
Cash

Cash is the most liquid and least volatile of all assets. For trustees, it is the most effective way of having funds ready to pay out benefits to members, as well as receiving new contributions. This will represent large sums of money. In 2006, pension funds allocated 5% of their assets to cash.

But, in holding money on deposit, returns are relatively low and there is no prospect of any capital growth. So it is worth looking at short-term cash instruments available through the money markets. These are designed for institutions, such as pension funds, as well as government and corporations, which have to manage large inflows and outflows of cash.

Excess funds can be deposited for a period as short as overnight. Other instruments might have a term of up to 12 months.

In seeking higher returns on their cash accounts, pension funds will not generally deal directly in the money market. Instead, they will invest in a fund that specialises in money markets, which will be expected to perform better than a benchmark related to the interest paid by banks. In this way, you should improve your returns without jeopardising your liquidity or touching your capital.

Interest rates

Interest rates are the basis on which the money markets operate. The Bank of England sets the base rate with a view to controlling inflation and managing the money supply.

For the money markets, however, the main benchmark is the wholesale rate at which banks lend short-term funds to each other. Known as LIBOR (London Interbank Offered Rate), it forms the contractual base for most transactions in the money markets.

The instruments

- 'Treasury bills' are the way in which the government manages its own requirements for cash in the short-term. They are generally issued in denominations with a face value of £5,000. An investor buys them at a discount. Instead of receiving interest, they will then be repaid in full after a term of between one and six months. The bills can be traded right up to the point when they mature.

- 'Certificates of deposit' (CDs) enable you to make savings for a set term with a fixed rate of interest. Although you cannot access your money directly until maturity, you can still sell your CD to another party, so raising cash immediately.

- 'Commercial paper' is an alternative means for corporations to manage their cash in the short-term, rather than taking out a loan with their bank. It allows them to raise money for up to 12 months from other participants in the money markets who have excess cash. Like treasury bills, commercial paper is issued at a rate lower than face value, which is then repaid in full on maturity.

NOTES

- 'Repurchase agreements' (repos) are when an organisation sells a security to another at a set price, then buys it back later, often overnight, at another price that includes interest.

High yield – a strategic asset class for pension funds

George Muzinich, President, Muzinich & Co. Inc

High yield corporate credit has a strategic role to play in pension portfolios. It can both enhance stability and add incremental returns.

High yield benefits from an arbitrary distinction dividing the world into two broad categories – the supposedly safe world of investment grade and the supposedly more perilous world of sub-investment grade. This creates inefficiency, which leads to opportunity. The current yield differential between BBB-, the lowest investment grade rating, and BB+, the highest sub-investment grade rating, is over 100 basis points.

It is important to clearly distinguish between credit risk and duration risk. High yield can be used as a strong cash generating anchor in the shorter end of the yield curve. It can enhance cash generation and help meet cash disbursement needs. Government bonds, rather than corporate bonds, should be used to help match long-term liabilities. General Motors was once an AAA rated credit.

High yield can act as an effective hedge against the inflation risk implicit in long dated government bonds. Our bond portfolios have about four years duration and our loan portfolios carry no duration risk. Inflation favors corporate borrowers. It allows them to pay back debt with currency that is less valuable. Inflation improves corporate cash flows and gives companies greater price flexibility in selling their goods and services.

High yield has, over more than sixteen years, provided*:

- Attractive inflation adjusted returns (over 5% per annum in the last 16 years).
- Strong risk adjusted performance (returns of approximately 10% p.a. with a volatility of about 6% and a Sharpe ratio of approximately 1 over the last 16 years).
- Low correlation to other asset classes (approximately 10% versus 10 year treasuries over the last 16 years).

High yield corporate credit should be part of a properly diversified asset management program.

Based on the Merrill Lynch US High Yield Constrained Cash Pay Index.

For more information please contact Thom Bentley, Director of Institutional Marketing:

Tel: +44 (0)20 7493 8018
Email: tbentley@muzinich.com

Alternatively, visit www.muzinich.com to find out more.

Muzinich & Co.

Part 3

Alternative assets

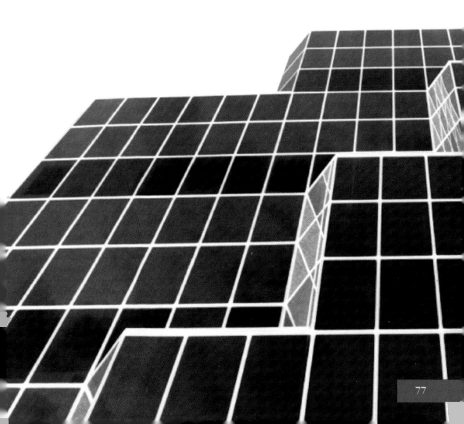

Chapter 9
Private equity

The capital gains from investing directly in private companies and maximising their potential can be spectacular. However, you can just as easily fail completely and be left with an asset worth nothing.

In this high-risk activity, private equity managers specialise in buying private companies in the belief that they can unlock their value in five to ten years, making a lucrative exit for their backers and for themselves by means of a trade sale or a flotation on the stock exchange.

Operating as private partnerships, private equity managers raise funds through a call for subscriptions, which they then invest in a portfolio of companies.

Historically, pension funds in the UK have steered clear of private equity as an asset because it involves tying up a large amount of money, usually a minimum of £5m, when the risks are immediate and the returns are uncertain and a long way off.

Although private equity might not fit comfortably into a pension's conventional model of matching assets and liabilities on a benchmarked, annual basis, it is now demanding the attention of trustees as an asset class for two powerful reasons:

1. Returns have proved consistently high over an extended period. According the British Venture

Capital Association, they have averaged 18.7% on an annual basis for the last ten years.

2. The behaviour of private equity as an asset is radically different from quoted equities and bonds, so it is proving an effective way of diversifying the overall risk profile of a pension fund.

However, it is a complex asset. The performance of different private equity managers varies dramatically. Gaining access to one of the top performers is hard, particularly if you are entering the market for the first time.

By definition, you will be putting your capital at risk. It is also going to be illiquid. Your money will be locked up for several years before you see any return. You cannot back out and you have to have the cash ready to meet any requests to draw down funds. Nor will you receive a regular income, as any profits will be re-invested in building a business or in paying off debt.

In the UK, under 1% of assets are generally allocated by pension funds to private equity. In the US, the figure is generally higher and in some funds reaches 10%.

Because returns are so lumpy, it is usually best to invest gradually in private equity, building up a commitment over a number of years, so evening out any fluctuations in performance. In that way, a pension fund will only be fully invested after ten years.

A further complication is that as capital is gradually drawn down as required to make acquisitions and cover expenses, pension funds can find that they are sitting on a lot of spare cash, which has been allocated, but not spent. So, it can be a better strategy to over-commit to make sure that capital is used efficiently.

NOTES

Investment vehicles

If your pension fund is large enough, you might choose to invest directly in private companies yourself, taking on the risks directly and relying on your own pool of expertise. Anyone with fewer resources is more likely to subscribe to one of the calls for funds by a specialist manager of private equity, such as 3i.

Operating as a closed-end fund, they will use the capital to invest in a portfolio of 20 to 30 companies. Alongside your capital, they will also probably take on high levels of debt, which can be used to offset tax against future profits.

These funds will focus on one of two main areas: venture capital or buy outs. Their performance depends heavily on each investment manager, who will be intensively involved in the future direction and control of each investment. Gaining access to these top performers is hard, so for pension funds making a start in private equity it often makes sense to invest in 'a fund of funds' run by a manager who knows the market.

Venture capital

In this type of private equity, funds are invested in new, innovative business, predominantly in IT, telecoms and life sciences. Typically, a stake is taken in one of the early rounds of finance. Many of these investments will fail. The returns are generated by the few that do well.

In assessing investments, private equity managers will look less at the scientific merits of a technology and more at its scope for commercial application.

Capital is usually only in the form of equity. As early-stage ventures have limited cashflow and minimal profits, there is little basis for meeting the commitments on a loan.

In the US, private equity is involved with ventures from even before they start to earn any revenue. In Europe, business angels are more likely to provide this seed capital with private equity becoming involved in later and larger rounds of finance.

Buy-outs

Buy-out funds target larger private companies with a longer trading record with a view to making a fundamental change in the way that the business operates, such as cutting costs, replacing the executive team, selling peripheral assets or merging with a competitor.

Because these changes are easier to make in a private company outside the scrutiny of financial markets, private equity is now bidding to make listed companies private with a view to transforming their value. Even major companies, such as Boots and Sainsburys, have become targets.

All these types of buy-out are heavily financed by debt, which allows tax to be offset against future profits. Returns on individual investment tend to be less extreme than in venture capital.

Costs

Because the role of the private manager is so central to the ultimate value of each investment, fees are higher than for more traditional asset classes. Normally 2% is charged on the capital committed plus a 20% share of any increase

NOTES

in the value of the assets. As a trustee you might want to ensure there is a clawback if other assets perform less well when they are sold later.

In return, you can expect the private equity manager to fulfil five main tasks:

1. Set the parameters of the portfolio

2. Find and screen acquisitions

3. Structure deals

4. Determine the strategic direction of companies acquired

5. Complete an exit from the investment.

To gain access to a wider spread of funds with a good track-record, you can invest through 'a funds of funds', although you will be adding another layer of cost, typically 1% on capital committed with the possibility of a percentage on gains.

Returns

For pension trustees, the main difficulty lies in committing to investments when returns cannot be measured on an annual basis and no benchmarks exist for comparing how their investments are doing.

Private equity managers will tell you that they are aiming to better the FTSE AllShare Index by 5% and will work internally towards an objective of doubling or tripling the value of their fund. Such sentiments do not sit easily in a model seeking to make an accurate match between assets and liabilities.

THE PENSION TRUSTEE'S INVESTMENT GUIDE

The only definite points for valuation are when capital is originally raised and when assets are finally sold. In the interim, you can measure the flow of cash in and out of the fund to give you an internal rate of return (IRR).

Expressed in this way, your returns will follow a J curve. In the first four to five years, returns will be negative as your committed capital is drawn down to invest in new assets and cover expenses. Thereafter you should start to see inflows as the value of assets is realised. Normally, you should see the benefits in cash, although you might be given quoted shares instead.

To track returns in the sector, it is probably best to follow an index as a proxy. For venture capital, it might be worth tracking the NASDAQ, which relies heavily on technology flotations, to give yourself a guide as to how the sector is performing.

In deciding how to allocate assets and in setting targets for private equity managers, you could also use a comparative tool, such as the Capital Asset Pricing Model, as a means of judging the additional premium that you should expect from private equity to compensate for its inherent illiquidity.

Hedge funds: No Longer the domain of the super-rich as pension funds see their worth

Liz Chong, Industry Analyst, EIM (United Kingdom) Ltd.

Unlike their US and Continental cousins, UK pension funds have shied away from investing in hedge funds. This has been to the detriment of UK pension funds, particularly with their extensive deficits. While these have narrowed in recent years due to the buoyant stock markets, the problem still remains.

Influential pension funds such as the BT pension scheme have sought to solve this by turning to alternative investments. The UK's largest pension fund with £38 billion of assets, the BT scheme is currently in the process of doubling its allocation to alternative investments to a sizeable 15%.

Hedge funds are an ideal vehicle for trustees because they can help pension funds meet their liabilities, offering diversification for portfolios that are dominated by equities or bonds.

They target absolute returns, i.e. their performances are not benchmarked to market indices. In a period where equities have slumped, investors will expect hedge funds to have protected themselves against market losses by using hedging strategies. This can be done by taking short positions to offset losses that would be incurred from positions that are exposed to the market's downslide.

At first glance, many tend to view the hedge fund industry as opaque and laden with risk. It is indeed easier to opt for the safety of US Treasuries or gilts than to dig into the mystique and the alarmist headlines in the press about hedge funds.

Hedge funds did certainly begin as the domain of the super-rich but the industry is certainly now entrenched within the financial world as it has been institutionalised. Hedge funds are high-profile and influential, taking stakes in some of the world's largest companies as they play an active role in pushing for deals to improve corporate profitability.

Assets under management in the hedge fund industry have soared from $39 billion in 1990 to $1.9 trillion in 2007.

The growth of the industry has been accelerated over the past decade by investments from influential pension funds, especially in the US – where hedge funds are no longer seen as the domain of the wealthy investor. Calpers, the largest US public pension fund, has been investing in hedge funds for five years.

In the UK, authorities also share the view of those across the Atlantic. This is underlined by the FSA's plans to allow the man on the street to invest in hedge funds – via the fund of hedge funds route. This will enable investors to spread their risk more widely beyond their usual choice of mutual funds as they add more value to their pension pots.

As a first step, investors usually opt for funds of hedge funds which are the best means of introduction to the industry. In doing this, investors can gain entry to a wide pool of hedge funds that they may not necessarily gain access to individually because of the high bar funds required for minimum investments. It enables investors to easily gain exposure to a range of hedge funds and different trading strategies without incurring the costs of researching the industry.

Funds of hedge funds also offer investors two choices: standardised products that have already been created to fit low, average or high risk appetites – or bespoke portfolios that are crafted to suit clients' demands.

For more information please contact:

EIM (United Kingdom) Limited
Devonshire House
Mayfair Place
London W1J 8AJ
Tel: +44 (0)20 7290 6100
Fax:+44 (0)20 7290 6101

Alternatively, visit www.eimgroup.com to find out more.

Yes, we are picky.

Chapter 10
Hedge funds

Hedge funds are designed to give a set annual return to investors regardless of whether financial markets are rising or falling. Organised as lightly regulated private partnerships, they use a full range of investment techniques to invest in securities, such as equities and bonds, as well as derivatives, to exploit any deviations from 'fair value' in capital markets.

Because they generally operate outside the regulatory control of mainstream financial centres, hedge funds can be more flexible than other asset managers in taking advantage of pricing anomalies. They are also unusual because they raise debt to fund their positions. In technical terms, they are 'leveraged': debt represents a relatively high proportion of their capital.

Since the early 1990s, hedge funds have grown rapidly as an alternative asset. Today, there are estimated to be 8,000 funds with $1.6 trillion under management.

According to an index produced by Credit Suisse Tremont, returns in 2006 were 13.9%. However, this figure hides wide variations in performance, as the best funds are making returns of 30% or 40%.

For pension trustees, who are under more pressure than ever to match their assets to their liabilities, the target returns and the relative lack of volatility offered by hedge funds are attractive, particularly as the link with how equities and bonds perform is low.

However, costs are high and investments are illiquid. An initial subscription to a fund usually requires a minimum of £1m. You will then pay 2% on your capital as a management charge plus 20% on any gains. On highly rated funds, these percentages might rise to 4% and 40%.

Because hedge funds take highly leveraged positions on predicting fine changes in the price of assets, the potential losses on any single investment can be total. However, as a trustee, it can be difficult to track your exposure. Hedge funds are often based offshore and they prefer to avoid having to disclose their exact mix of investment techniques.

Unlike other pooled vehicles, such as unit trusts, there is also usually a cap on the size of a hedge fund before it starts to distort the market in which it is operating.

Investment techniques

Originally, hedge funds were developed 50 years ago to protect investors against downturns in the market by selling 'short', as well as buying 'long'.

Conventional long positions are when you buy an asset in the expectation that it will appreciate in value. Taking a negative position, or shorting, is when you expect the price of an asset to fall. You sell a security that you do not own, then buy it back once the price has fallen.

To take short positions, hedge funds often borrow securities from pension schemes. Such 'stock lending' can be a profitable sideline, as long as it is permitted under the deed of trust.

NOTES

Because hedge funds have the option of either going long or short, they can act on both positive and negative views, so doubling their opportunities for making a return. Typically, they will take both short and long positions on assets, such as bonds, exploiting any deviations in value at different points in the yield curve.

Similarly, they will invest in derivatives, such as futures, to guard against adverse movements in the market – or to double their potential return. Alternatively, hedge funds will use arbitrage, simultaneously buying and selling an asset, to exploit any mismatches in prices.

Because they take on debt, hedge funds can take concentrated positions, so taking advantage of relatively small movements in price.

Investment strategies

Also sometimes known as 'absolute return' funds, because they expect to make a return regardless of the volatility of capital markets, hedge funds rely heavily on their managers having the freedom and the flexibility to exercise their skills in deploying a full range of investment techniques. The unconstrained nature of their activities results in a multiplicity of investment strategies. However, hedge funds can be broadly broken down into four types:

1. 'Relative value' is when hedge funds exploit mismatches in the price of securities based on the same underlying asset. They will typically take short and long positions against forecast returns.

2. 'Event driven' is when hedge funds focus on corporate activities, such as acquisitions, restructuring or

liquidations, which can result in major changes in value.

3. 'Equity hedging' is where superior returns are sought by going in long undervalued assets and short in overvalued ones. Hedge funds will often look at distressed securities, which are typically illiquid or close to insolvency.

4. 'Trading funds' have a top-down approach to global assets, such as currencies, commodities, equities or bonds. Computer models are often used to identify opportunities, determining the size and timing of an investment.

Each of these categories varies in its level of volatility and correlation to other assets. Given the discreet basis on which hedge funds operate, it can be difficult for pension schemes to decide in which fund to invest. It generally makes more sense to gain initial exposure by investing in a fund of funds, which has a good understanding of the market and good access to high performers. You will add an extra 1% to your management charge, as well as a 5% – 10% slice of any capital gain, but it does reduce any risk of making a mistake. Since 1990, according to Bloomberg, funds of hedge funds have cumulatively returned an average of 10% a year.

Structuring and operating funds

John Trustram Eve, Partnership Incorporations Ltd (PIL)

PIL is one of the leading companies in the UK market at establishing and operating collective investment schemes. It particularly specialises in the property market. The setting up, promotion, operation and winding up of a Collective Investment Scheme ('CIS') constitute regulated activities. Consequently, a person authorised under FSMA must conduct these activities. PIL is regulated and authorised by the Financial Services Authority to provide such regulated activities and also to provide investment advice.

PIL is independent of any bank, agent, firm of surveyors, financial institutions and even its owners.

PIL possesses considerable experience in designing fund structures, identifying investors, managing the fund launch process and managing the regulatory and administrative aspects once a fund is launched. PIL acts for both institutional and private equity investors.

The work PIL carries out has proven to shorten the time it takes to launch a vehicle; to ensure that technical/structural problems are identified and resolved as early as possible. This enables asset managers/sponsors to reduce overheads and to minimise the diversion of management time to administration.

Our initial role is one of project managing the launch. Whilst launching a fund looks straightforward, history shows that there are difficulties lurking most of the way so that experience pays. What is required is a logical progression through the requirements and practical experience of the application of the regulations.

At present funds fall into two distinct categories: those designed for institutional investors and those for individuals. However, we now believe that we can produce a means by which ordinary investors, putting around £25,000 to £50,000 into each investment, can become invested in the much larger funds designed for institutions, where minimum investments are usually £5 million. We are expecting to launch our own such fund towards the end of 2007/early 2008. This generally improves the spread of risk as well as providing a solid organisation with whom to join.

Operating a fund looks straightforward enough. Single asset funds generally do not raise many issues other than when to sell, and the relevant judgments and forecasting concerning not only the market, but also tax. Funds which benefit from tax allowances or special tax treatment, such as film funds, require particularly careful handling and very good record-keeping. Similarly, with on-shore funds relying upon off-shore investments or vice versa, precise record-keeping and administration are required to evidence proper management control (in the correct jurisdiction) to reduce tax leakage.

The independence of the operation of a fund from its sponsors therefore has its advantages. A number of funds PIL operates have sponsors who have ample expertise and experience to both launch and operate funds, however they have seen it necessary or advantageous to use PIL as the operator. The operator is able to deal more easily with conflicts of interest between the sponsors and the investors, leaving the sponsors to concentrate their management time on assets rather than administration. They can also take advantage of PIL's experience and expertise to reduce launch and administration costs, and to maximise returns to investors.

The demand from investors has been very strong in the last few years, while opportunities for investing in UK property have become increasingly scarce. The inevitable result has been the well-known reduction in returns, as well as the difficulty of finding a suitable product at all. The combination of these trends has led to both sponsors and investors looking elsewhere than UK property to try and obtain better returns.

This search has of itself, led to an explosion of funds investing in European property. In practice, while the opportunities look significant, actually finding investments which are predictable and provide better returns to investors is proving as challenging as investing in the UK. Not because of a lack of product itself, but finding properties which are clean and have real prospects of growth in value. In our experience, unless the sponsor has knowledgeable staff on the ground in the relevant localities, not only to find the right opportunities but also to manage them proactively, there is a real risk they will not prove over time to be the investments they were thought to be.

For more information please contact:

John Trustram Eve, Chairman of Partnership Incorporations Ltd
Tel: +44 (0)20 7839 9730
Email: john@pincs.com

Alternatively, visit www.pincs.com to find out more.

Do your pensions have adequate exposure to Property?

Have you exploited the opportunities provided by Collective Investment Schemes?

PIL are one of the largest independent organisation Launching and Operating Collective Investment Schemes. Independent of agents, banks and other financial institutions.

If you want to go further then talk to us to see how we can help with existing or new purpose designed scheme.

Please contact us

Telephone 020 7839 9730   E-mail info@pincs.com

Suite 101A, 3 Whitehall Court, London SW1A 2EL

Flexible
Independent
Professional

Partnership Incorporations Limited is authorised and regulated by The Financial Services Authority

Chapter 11
Commodities

Commodities are being re-discovered as an asset class. After a flat market in the 1980s and 1990s, prices for raw materials, such as oil, copper and gold, are surging on the back of demand in Asia and interest round the world is growing in bio-fuels made from crops.

Prices can be highly volatile, but the overall return on the market is similar to equities. For pension trustees, the additional attraction is that commodities behave differently from other assets. By including them in a portfolio, you can reduce your exposure to risk without affecting your performance.

As direct physical inputs to goods, commodities are closely linked to changes in economic conditions. In the event of a rise in inflation or a natural disaster, they will rise in price, rather than fall like any other asset.

More generally, commodities have a negative correlation to equities, so they tend to do well when financial markets are falling and less well when they are rising. For pension trustees, it means that they can be a good way of evening out how their scheme performs year by year.

Commodities also differ from alternative assets. Unlike private equity or hedge funds, any capital invested is highly liquid and management fees can be low as 0.75%, although transaction costs are usually high, as contracts are frequently traded.

The market

Generally defined as standard goods that, like a barrel of oil, a bar of gold or a bushel of wheat, can be exchanged like for like, commodities break down into three broad categories: energy, metals and agricultural.

Between 2002 and 2006, the International Monetary Fund's index of primary commodity prices leapt a total of 126%. Energy led the way with oil up 80% and gas (in Europe) up 108%. Amongst agricultural commodities, wheat rose 45%, cocoa 30% and bananas 48%.

Most dramatic was the performance of metals, such as copper (+162%), zinc (+246%) and uranium (+656%).

But not all commodities have done as well: olive oil and lamb have fallen slightly in price, and coffee costs much the same at it did in 1990.

Such highs and lows are typical of commodities. Because it takes so long for new production to come on line or to close down, they are highly sensitive to changes in demand.

The contracts

Most investors steer clear of buying commodities directly, because the complications of storage and distribution are too great. The exception for pension funds is gold, which has been a traditional reserve against adverse economic conditions. After hitting a low in 2002, it has risen 70% in value in the last five years, returning 14% in 2006 alone.

Apart from gold, as an investor you are more likely to buy a futures contract, which has existed in one form or another for centuries. It is designed as a form of price insur-

NOTES

ance for producers, who have put their resources into sowing a crop or sinking a well and want to guard against a sudden drop in price when they come to sell months or years later. Similarly, users of commodities would like to avoid any unexpected rise in what they have to pay between placing the order and settling their account.

Futures essentially supply the capital to balance the books: the investor agrees now to buy and sell the commodity at a set price on the date when it is due for delivery. Contracts can last from three months to five years and are traded on exchanges (such as the Chicago Mercantile Exchange and LIFFE), which are live auctions based on the latest information on supply and demand.

As an investor, you can take an informed view of whether the cash price for a commodity is likely to increase. But futures also offer you other ways of making a return, which is why historically they have performed so much better as an asset than just the market or 'spot' price for commodities.

You can charge producers a risk premium for guaranteeing their price on delivery. As a future nears completion, it trades closer and closer to the quoted market price. So investors usually sell or 'roll' their nearer term contracts into longer term ones, on which they can still command a healthy risk premium. This process of rolling forward contracts is frequently called 'backwardation'.

Because futures are settled on delivery of the commodity, you do not have to pay anything when you enter into a contract. Your role is to make sure the books balance at the end. But you will have to set aside an amount as collateral, which in the meantime can be invested in the money markets, giving you an extra source of return.

Trading the index

The volatility of individual commodities means that only the largest or the boldest pension schemes will trade them in directly through a futures broker. More probably, you will be looking for exposure to a basket of different commodities.

The two principal benchmarks are the Dow Jones AIG Commodity Index and the Goldman Sachs Commodity Index. Both invest in 20 to 25 different types of commodity, buying futures near completion and putting the principal into the money markets. Where they differ is that Goldman Sachs bases its allocation on production levels over the last five years, which means that it is as much as 80% exposed to energy, whereas Dow Jones caps any one commodity at 15%.

To track these benchmarks passively, investors can buy the underlying futures themselves or subscribe to a specialist fund which mimics the index through the use of derivatives.

For a more active approach, you can invest in a unit trust that takes equity positions directly in commodity producers or you could consider buying into an Exchange Traded Fund. These are a relatively new type of quoted product which allow groups of investors to invest in commodities through an equity vehicle. So far, they have mainly been used for gold and silver but are starting to expand into oil, other metals and crops.

Morgan Stanley

Thinking about your allocation to alternatives? So are we.

Adding alternative investments to an existing portfolio of traditional assets can bring clear benefits.

But it takes real skill to determine which asset categories, and in what quantity, to add. Hedge funds, private equity, real estate, infrastructure, senior loans, currencies, commodities, GTAA, CDOs – the list goes on. Also, the risks of alternative investments can be qualitatively different from conventional assets, making the modelling of alternative assets a non-trivial exercise. And the implementation of such a portfolio also poses major hurdles, as the diversity of the assets adds significant complexity to operations, risk management, reporting, due diligence and portfolio oversight.

That's why **Morgan Stanley Investment Management** has designed the Diversified Portfolio Allocation – Alternatives (DPAA) programme. The service provides our clients with a one-stop solution for adding alternatives to their portfolios and ranges from bespoke design of the investment strategy all the way through to integrated implementation or a pooled fund solution.

To discuss these issues further, please contact
Richard Lockwood (Tel: 020 7425 9193 Email: Richard.Lockwood@morganstanley.com)
Ian Martin (Tel: 020 7425 3473 Email: Ian.Martin@morganstanley.com)
Simone Bouch (Tel: 020 7425 8776 Email: Simone.Bouch@morganstanley.com)
Peter Escott (Tel: 020 7425 4673 Email: Peter.Escott@morganstanley.com)

Making an allocation to alternatives

Richard Lockwood, Head of UK Business, MSIM

It is generally accepted that alternative assets have a role to play in well constructed portfolios by delivering diversification and enhancing the portfolios risk/return profile. While the potential benefits of these investments may be clear, there are a number of areas for pension schemes that their trustees need to consider before investing including; what is an alternative asset, which alternatives are suitable for your scheme and finally what are the potential implementation issues?

Rather than thinking that alternative assets are just hedge funds, private equity, infrastructure one should identify them as strategies either where the returns are driven by manager skill (alpha) or as strategies that are different to the existing assets held within the portfolio. Research suggests that marked improvements in a portfolio's characteristics can be achieved by investing part into a well-diversified mix of alternatives. However, the logistics of investing and monitoring these assets, coupled with the governance burden, could make diversification into alternatives impractical for many schemes. This is why trustees need to identify managers who have the capability to identify the correct set of alternatives for their scheme's portfolio. One solution is to effectively outsource this whole process to those asset managers with the necessary range of skills, who can then create investment structures which deliver a single point of investment to schemes. This means that the burden of risk management and governance now falls to the asset manager.

We believe that many pension schemes and their trustees could benefit from the diversification and risk/return characteristics which a diversified portfolio of alternatives could bring. However, some schemes have been prevented from making such investments because of major administrative, governance and risk management burdens that making these investments individually would bring. Asset manager-led solutions which combine asset allocation and modelling skills, together with a broad range of underlying alternatives strategies, would seem to be the perfect solution.

For more information please contact:

Richard Lockwood, Executive Director
Morgan Stanley Investment Management
20 Bank Street, Canary Wharf, London E14 4AD
Tel: +44 (0)20 7425 9193 • Fax: +44 (0)20 7425 7832
Email: Richard.Lockwood@morganstanley.com

Chapter 12
Infrastructure

For trustees looking for a dependable source of long-term income, the infrastructure is fast emerging as an asset in its own right.

For essential services, such as hospitals, roads, power stations, airports and water, governments in North America and Europe, as well as emerging markets like China and India, accept that they can no longer rely wholly on tax receipts. Instead, they are turning to capital markets either to sell off utilities or to raise funding through public private partnerships.

The potential is huge. Around the world, only a small proportion of infrastructure assets operate under a capital structure that accepts private investment.

To meet the growing demand for capital, large-scale specialist funds have been formed, first in Australia and Canada but now also in the UK. By the end of 2006 as much as $150bn had been raised worldwide, according to the credit agency Standard & Poor's.

Asset qualities

By their nature, infrastructure assets are built for the long-term. The initial costs of constructing a hospital or an airport are high, but the facility will last for decades, occupying a strongly protected competitive position, if not a monopoly. Once in operation, running costs are relatively low and margins are high. The result for investors is a predictable future stream of income, which as a regulated service should be proofed against inflation.

For pension trustees these are attractive characteristics. On the right investment, returns can be as high as equities with volatility as low as bonds. In addition, as infrastructure is usually an essential service, its performance is not linked too closely to the economic cycle (except perhaps in the case of transport) and its correlation to other assets is low.

Risks

However, there are risks. Because the upfront costs are so high, these types of project generally have high levels of debt, often totalling 80% of capital, so investors can find themselves exposed when interest rates change. If refinancing then occurs, they could find their position is diluted. Because interest in the sector has been so high in the last two years, deals are becoming more highly leveraged and the overall quality of credit is declining.

As essential services, these assets are usually regulated. Any changes in policy or enforcement can be damaging. Investors will find that they have to strike a balance in deciding where to pursue opportunities.

In markets such as the UK, where there is long experience of involving the capital markets in the infrastructure, regulatory practices are well established, but many of the best assets have already gone. So it might be worth looking at new markets in Europe, even if the regulatory framework for utilities is less established.

NOTES

Channels

For investors, the choice usually lies between buying shares in infrastructure companies or subscribing to corporate bonds. Generally, they will act on an indirect basis, because the level of returns depends on a specialised knowledge of each particular sector and on an active management of the risks.

Pension funds will either subscribe to a listed fund or participate in an unlisted joint vehicle, purposely designed for institutional investors such as themselves. Smaller schemes might look at Exchange Traded Funds as a lower cost and more liquid way of accessing the market.

However, like property, trustees might choose to fund an infrastructure project either by themselves or acting in a consortium, which cuts out any charges and gives them direct exposure to future streams of income.

Distressed debt

Howard S. Marks, Chairman,
Oaktree Capital Management

Is investing in distressed debt a good thing?

That's a trick question.

Like all other assets classes and investment strategies, buying distressed debt is a great idea when it can be done at prices that are far below intrinsic value, whereas at other times it can produce lackluster results.

Like everything else in the world of investing, success with distressed debt is a matter of opportunity and execution

Over the eighteen years of my involvement with distressed debt, there have been two periods when it was possible to access highly outstanding returns through bargain-basement purchases. There have also been times when buying opportunities were nothing special. And yet high absolute results have been achieved across periods (and, I think, achieved with the risks solidly under control).

The ability to invest in distressed debt at low prices depends first on the creation of an ample supply

Historically, that supply has come into existence when a period of lax lending has been followed by a period of both fundamental and psychological weakness.

From time to time, the capital markets will approach a cyclical high in terms of generosity and a low in terms of discernment and discipline. Confidence comes to outweigh caution. Providers of capital compete to buy securities and make loans. And the way they compete is by accepting less in terms of debt coverage and loan covenants. In other words, they settle for a skimpy margin of safety. Credit standards are pushed to the point where many borrowers will be unable to service their debt if conditions in the environment deteriorate, as inevitably will become the case at some point.

When things in the economic and business worlds are going swimmingly and investors are in firm grasp of their composure, few forced or motivated sellers crowd the exits, and thus there are few bargains. But when negatives accumulate in the environment, investors often become unable to hold on (for legal, organizational, economic or psychological reasons) and bargains can become rife. Oftentimes these influences can be seen most clearly in the market for distressed debt, as that is where the extremes of the cycles in corporate creditworthiness and investor psychology are reached.

1990 witnessed a recession, a credit crunch, the Gulf War, the melt-down of many of the prominent LBOs of the 1980s, and the government's war on junk bonds. The accumulation of these events had tangible effects on creditworthiness (for example, the default rate on high yield bonds reached 10 percent) and a very negative effect on debtholders' psyches. Investors are usually happy to hold unbesmirched assets marked at high prices, but they can become entirely unwilling to deal with them when flaws become evident and their prices are brought low. This is the process that generates opportunities for bargains – in distressed debt as elsewhere. And this is what happened in 1990.

Likewise, in 2002 we also saw a recession and credit crunch, this time along with the invasion of Afghanistan, the collapse of the telecom industry, and the disclosure of corporate scandals beginning with Enron and eventually affecting several other companies. Again we witnessed the corrosive effects of fundamental deterioration and psychological undermining. The default rate on high yield bonds once again soared past 10 percent, and downgrades turned holders of the debt of many former high grade companies – now 'fallen angels' – into highly motivated sellers. As had been the case in 1990, purchases of distressed debt made in 2002 had the potential to produce ultra-high rates of return.

So, is it all wine and roses?

No, because these helpful influences are not everlasting (remember, the things that are good for most investors, and most citizens, are bad for those looking for bargains in distressed debt). In 1996, for example, the economy was strong, business was good, capital markets were wide open (willing to solve overextended companies' financial problems), and investors and creditors were fat and happy. There were no depressing influences and no forced sellers. As a result, there were few chances to buy distressed debt capable of producing the returns investors long for.

There is no silver bullet in investing – not even distressed debt. The profit opportunity is cyclical, rising and falling as described above. Potential distressed debt supply is created through the unwise extension of credit and turned into actual supply when conditions deteriorate. But at other times, usually after a round of losses has punished investors and lenders and left them chastened, discipline in credit standards reasserts itself and the supply of potential distressed debt contracts. So, distressed debt investing can be highly profitable at some times, but certainly not all.

So where do we stand today?

In the last few years and even as recently as July, there was little to do in the world of distressed debt. The combination of a salutary economic environment and generous capital markets enabled most companies to compile good performance – and even allowed the few underperformers to finance their way out of trouble. Defaults among high yield bonds ran at a 25-year low, and very little debt became distressed.

By now the events of mid-summer 2007 have become well known. As delinquencies among subprime mortgages rose, as it became clear that loans had been made to borrowers who were not creditworthy, rising interest rates posed a burden that these weak borrowers would be unable to meet and the prices of the homes serving as collateral were declining. These developments caused numerous downgrades among residential mortgaged-backed securities underlaid by subprime mortgages. These downgrades rippled through collateralized debt obligations and hedge funds owning subprime assets, bringing margin calls and concern about capital withdrawals. Difficulty in valuing and selling subprime securities led to a few meltdowns, and thus the need to sell cascaded into other asset classes. The sum of the above produced widespread worry – particularly in cases where investors had used short-term borrowings to leverage assets that were now viewed as illiquid and risky. The principal impact in the corporate debt arena has been with regard to hundreds of billions of dollars of financing for buyouts that banks had promised to provide under terms which are no longer acceptable to investors. The banks seem likely to accept price reductions – and the resultant losses – to move this debt off their balance sheets.

Many markets have been infected with contagion related to these deteriorating psychological and technical conditions – considerations that negatively affect the supply and demand for securities without reference to their fundamental quality. But the fundamental quality of corporate debt seems generally unimpaired at present. The economy is still healthy and companies are performing well. The impact on distressed debt investors likewise has been psychological rather than fundamental – but for the positive. While the incidence of distress has not risen, distressed debt investors are encouraged that the recent events provide a reminder of the way in which – once fundamentals weaken – non-fundamental factors can spread distress throughout the debt market. Little distress exists today, but investors believe the conditions for its growth can be achieved, and thus that an incident of elevated returns from distressed debt may be nearer at hand than had been thought only recently.

Even when conditions become good for distressed debt investing, performance still cannot be accomplished without deft execution

Compared to buying mainstream stocks and bonds, distressed debt investing is certainly a 'skill position'. Judgments have to be made about the survivability, prospects and value of an enterprise in crisis, and about the legal and *realpolitik* restructuring process that will reset an overly indebted company's balance sheet and usually turn many creditors into owners. These judgments have to be made from the outside – there are no dog-and-pony shows, due diligence rooms or meetings with helpful corporate executives – and often at a time when financial information is in short supply and possibly of questionable validity.

As with other forms of so-called alternative investing, the range of returns among distressed debt investors at a given time is probably much wider than it is among participants in the more efficient mainstream stock and bond markets. Personal investing skill based on aptitude and experience – 'alpha' – is the essential ingredient. Inefficient markets may make mispriced securities available, but they do not hold up a sign pointing the way to the best bargains. Distressed debt investing from time to time provides investment opportunities with great potential, but the outcome will always be dependent on skillful execution.

Howard S. Marks, Chairman, Oaktree Capital Management, CFA, CIC

Mr. Marks was a pioneer in the management of high yield bonds and convertible securities and co-founded Oaktree Capital Management in 1995. Previously, Mr. Marks headed a department at The TCW Group, Inc. which managed investments in high yield bonds, convertible securities and distressed debt. He was also Chief Investment Officer for Domestic Fixed Income of Trust Company of the West and President of TCW Asset Management Company. Before joining TCW, Mr. Marks was with Citicorp Investment Management for 16 years where, from 1978 to 1985, he served as vice president and manager of the convertible and high yield bond portfolios. Earlier, he was an equity analyst and the bank's Director of Investment Research. Mr. Marks holds a BSEc. degree cum laude from The Wharton School at the University of Pennsylvania with a major in Finance and an MBA in Accounting and Marketing from the Graduate School of Business of the University of Chicago.

For more information please contact Anis Adel:

Tel: +44 (0)20 7201 4600
Email: aadel@oaktreecapital.com

Alternatively, visit www.oaktreecapital.com

Part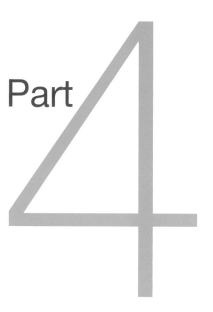

Derivatives

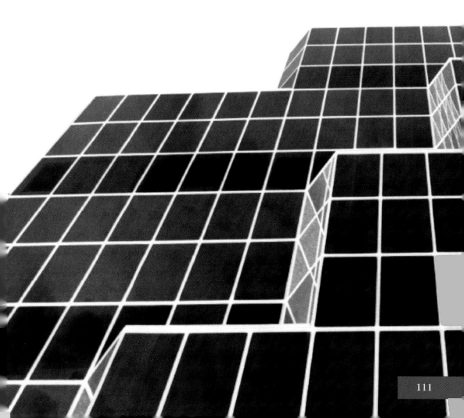

Chapter 13

Risk instruments

For pension trustees, derivatives enjoy a mixed reputation. In the press, they usually appear as speculative bets on the future direction of markets that result in huge gains or losses on relatively small movements in prices. More often than not, it seems that derivatives are the shadow lurking behind any crisis on the world's financial markets.

While it is true that they can be a highly effective means of quickly gaining exposure to volatile markets at little initial cost, that is not their original purpose as a risk instrument. For you as a trustees, if managed in line with your overall investment strategy, derivatives can be a fast, cheap and efficient way of matching your flows of cash, adjusting your portfolio at low cost and nudging up your returns. Essentially, they are tools that give pension schemes more precision in managing the risk profile.

It is a point that more and more trustees are taking. In a survey by Mercer Consulting in July 2007, nearly a fifth of pension schemes in the UK said that they were using derivatives to manage their liabilities, which was three times more than a year previously.

What they are

Like insurance, derivates are a way of guarding against loss. Instead of covering plant and equipment, you are limiting the exposure of financial assets, such as equities, bonds, commodities and cash, to volatility in prices and interest rates.

Based on an underlying asset, derivatives are contracts in which two parties are able to exchange their risks. So, for instance, a farmer can be sure in advance of earning a set price for a crop, while the buyer knows what they are going to have to pay. To make sure the books balance on the delivery date, an investor will underwrite the contract.

Working in the same way, borrowers can fix the cost of their lending, exporters can peg their exchange rate and manufacturers can avoid any sudden hikes in the cost of their inputs. Similarly, pension schemes can protect themselves against unexpected fluctuations in the value of their securities or they can make tactical adjustments to their portfolios.

The advantage of using derivatives in this way is that the capital required upfront is minimal and the cost of transactions is low. Instead of having to buy and sell securities, derivatives can be used to mimic the performance of the underlying asset.

For professional investors, these attributes make derivatives an attractive investment in their own right, particularly as money can be borrowed to take large positions in volatile markets that might otherwise be difficult to access. The downside is that losses can quickly escalate.

As a result, trustees may be restricted from using derivatives under their deed of trust. In any case, given the long-term nature of schemes, particular care should be taken in overseeing their use.

In practice, there are two principal applications for derivatives in pension schemes: to create a better match between assets and liabilities; and to improve performance and to reduce risk in the management of funds.

The market

The market for derivatives is huge. The amount outstanding on contracts at the end of 2006 was some $450,000bn.

There are two ways of buying and selling derivatives. One is through standard contracts on exchanges such as the Chicago Mercantile Exchange or Euronext.Liffe. These are highly liquid with thousands of trades per hour, so giving a pinpoint read on market sentiment. Contracts are generally for a fixed period and are at a set size.

Although you do not have to make a payment upfront, the risk of credit failure is made through a cash deposit which can be adjusted on a daily basis if losses accumulate.

The alternative is to make a direct arrangement with a counterparty. Usually arranged by investment banks over the counter (OTC), i.e. through their own network of dealers rather than through a formal exchange, this market can accommodate any particular set of requirements.

In managing their financial exposure through derivatives on these markets, trustees will come across them in three principal forms: futures, swaps and options.

Derivatives Education

Fresh thinking

Liffe.SM

NYSE Euronext

Find out more from the experts

In today's fast-moving capital markets, professional education is essential to keep a step ahead of the competition.

Our education programme offers a wide range of courses on derivatives covering the key areas of Commodities, Equities and Interest Rates.

Our courses are ideal for pension fund trustees and employees of banks, securities houses, funds and all institutions interested in, or already using derivatives. Courses are also divided by asset, so delegates can learn in an environment which focuses on their area of interest.

For more information on the courses, including prices, dates, speaker profiles and course content, please go to www.euronext.com/education

Alternatively, call +44 (0)20 7379 2200 or email education@liffe.com

Why invest in Asia?

Robert Lloyd George founded Lloyd George Management (LGM) as an Asian and Global Emerging Markets investment specialist in Hong Kong in 1991.

The firm has expanded its operations over the years with the opening of five other regional offices where its 28 portfolio managers and analysts are based.

In 1993 LGM opened a representative office in Mumbai to provide company research on the Indian equity market (one of the first foreign investment houses permitted to do so). In 1995 LGM opened an office in London to provide fund management and research on global emerging markets. In 1998 LGM opened an office in Florida to better focus its research efforts in Latin America. In 2001 an office was opened in Singapore and, in 2006, in Tokyo to strengthen its coverage of the Japan market.

LGM continues to specialise in Asia and emerging markets and is now considered a medium-sized, independent 'boutique' managing over US$15bn in these markets.

Here, Lloyd George Management Chairman and CEO, Robert Lloyd George, describes why investing in Asia is attractive…

The case for Asia today is a strong but simple one. It is based on higher economic growth, political stability, high savings rates, a strong work ethic and the visible shift of wealth and capital to the countries of the Far East and of South Asia. China is of course the main motor of growth and demand, which affects all its trading partners and Asian neighbours. Among these we may also include Australia, which occupies an important part in our Asia Pacific portfolios and whose economy is largely driven by the high level of exports to Asia, specifically to China. The price of many raw materials and commodities, including oil and gas, minerals and soft commodities such as wool, cotton and foodstuffs is now being driven at the margin by the increased demand by consumers in China and India. India is perhaps 15 years behind China in the development of the middle class and also in its national infrastructure spending, which affect the demand for these natural resources.

We believe that this trend will continue for another 10-15 years. The financial strength of Asia is also apparent in the high foreign exchange reserves and a strong surplus on trade and current accounts, which is a striking change from the situation in 1997/98, when most countries were running deficits and the currencies fell sharply against the US dollar. Today we see many Asian currencies showing steady annual appreciation against the US dollar, reflecting these strong fundamentals. This further underlines the case for investing in Asia.

We have a good selection of companies and sectors in the Asia Pacific region across our portfolios, including not only the natural resources in Australia and New Zealand, plantations in Malaysia and Indonesia, but also the strong manufacturing and commercial groups based in Hong Kong and Singapore. Most major Chinese companies are now listed in Hong Kong and among the big capitalisation groups are the Chinese telecoms, banks and oil companies. Technology is mainly represented by Taiwan and Korea, although we now have a growing software sector in India. Our Indian portfolios are dominated by the banking, cement, telecoms, software and energy sectors. The Indian listed companies have recorded now for two years over 30% annual earnings-per-share growth, and this is perhaps the strongest argument for including these important new emerging markets in Asia (India and China), which are over US$1 trillion in size.

Finally, the argument for valuation remains compelling, based on this strong underlying growth, and the fact that price to book and price to earnings ratios remain significantly lower than in the developed markets of Europe and North America, whilst many companies are now managing their capital more efficiently to the benefit of shareholders.

In conclusion, we see the economic arguments allied to the strengthening currencies and relatively lower risk profile compared to a decade ago as being the most salient arguments for investing in Asia today. It is always better to take a long-term view, as we learn from the current volatility in world markets.

R. Lloyd George

Robert Lloyd George
31st August 2007

For more information:

Tel: +44 (0)20 7408 7688
Email: info@uk.lloydgeorge.com

Alternatively, visit www.lloydgeorge.com

LLOYD GEORGE MANAGEMENT

LLOYD GEORGE MANAGEMENT

Lloyd George Management

•

Specialist Investors

•

Asia and Global Emerging Markets

•

Pension Funds, Governments, Charities & Foundations

For more information please contact:

Natasha Airey

Email: info@uk.lloydgeorge.com

Chapter 14
Futures

The technique of managing price risks with futures began in the grain markets of North America in the 19th century. By agreeing a set price well in advance of the harvest, buyers and sellers could remove the economic dangers of facing a glut or a shortage if they waited until market day.

The futures exchange in Chicago is still a world leader along with Euronext.Liffe in London. Today these markets trade in a wide range of commodities, as well as in equities, bonds, currencies and interest rates.

Rarely, if ever, do these futures involve the actual delivery of goods. They are contractual instruments for balancing the books. Although ultimately their value depends on an underlying asset, they are highly liquid markets in their own right. Thousands of trades are executed a minute, making futures a sensitive and accurate measure of pricing levels.

Although futures can be treated as high-risk, high-yield investments, for pension trustees, they primarily represent a technique for hedging their liabilities and for making tactical adjustment to their portfolios.

The futures contract

In capital-intensive industries like farming or mining, futures allow producers to lock in a market price, before they start committing their resources. Terms are generally for three months, but could stretch to five years. As the other party to the contract, buyers of these inputs can remove the threat of any sudden fluctuations in price.

If these agreements are made directly (or over the counter) through an intermediary, they are known as 'forwards'. If, as is more likely, they are traded in standard units of time, quantity and quality through a central exchange, they are called 'futures'.

On entering a futures contract, you make a small deposit into an account at the exchange. Usually referred to as 'a margin', it amounts to between 5% and 10%, although it can be more if trading conditions are volatile. As prices fluctuate for the underlying asset in the spot markets, adjustments are made to your account. If losses are being made, then you will be called for a top up.

When the contract ends, the initial margin is refunded with any gains added or losses deducted. As a result, when buyers and sellers then enter the spot market for delivery of goods, these adjustments ensure that the originally agreed price still applies regardless of what has subsequently happened on the market.

Hedging

As well as grains and minerals, futures can be a useful tactic for pension schemes in limiting or hedging their risks.

Futures can be used to re-balance an equity or bond portfolio in either taking a long (positive) view or short (negative) view. Futures work well in the short-term, particularly as the costs of entry and exit are so low. But in the longer term, it is usually more efficient to buy the underlying security, as maturities on futures often last no longer than three months.

For managing exposures on international securities, forwards on foreign exchange are widely used. Futures are also an attractive way of overlaying the risks in tracking an index. Rather than buying or selling securities, it is easier to go long or short in the futures market. This is particularly attractive in modifying the duration of a bond portfolio.

Returns

To investors, particularly of hedge funds, futures can be an attractive way of quickly gaining exposure to markets. For a small initial deposit, a significant financial position is quickly gained, either in expectation that prices will rise or fall. This high degree of leverage means that any gains or losses are greatly magnified. Even if the movement in the price of a future is small, in comparison to the initial deposit, it will be substantial. So, even relatively minor events in the market can have a dramatic impact.

A less risky way of investing is through 'spreads', where you spot variations in price between futures on different goods or on different exchanges. The most common technique is to trade on the risk premium in futures.

As a contract nears completion, the price of a future converges with the spot market and the risk premium disappears. So as an investor, you sell the future and buy one on a longer maturity, which has a higher risk premium and is trading at a discount. In a futures portfolio, such a rollover is standard, although it will add to transaction costs.

Controls

Whether pension funds are directly or indirectly exposed to futures, proper controls on their use should be in place. If used well, they are a highly effective instrument for managing portfolio risk. If used speculatively, the gains can be spectacular, but trustees should be aware that any capital invested is at risk of total loss.

Pictet Asset Management Limited

Rod Hearn, Chief Marketing Officer

Daniel Sear, Head of Business Development
United Kingdom

Pictet Asset Management (PAM) is the institutional investment management arm of Pictet & Cie. Founded in 1805, Pictet & Cie is one of Europe's leading and longest established private banks. It is wholly owned by eight partners.

PAM includes all the operating subsidiaries and divisions of the Group responsible for institutional asset management. Our mission is to provide world-class performance and services to our clients through dedication to excellence in all aspects of asset management.

PAM enjoys a global reach, extending from Geneva, London, Frankfurt, Milan, Madrid, Paris and Zurich to Tokyo, Singapore, Hong Kong, Dubai and Montreal.

PAM first began managing institutional clients in the 1960s. Assets managed by PAM amount to over USD114bn (June 07), sourced from blue chip clients globally. Our clients include pension funds, mutual funds, financial institutions and family offices in the UK and worldwide.

We are committed to long-term organic growth. We can afford to take a long-term view because we have no outside shareholders. There is no pressure from third parties to meet short-term growth targets and no issues with takeovers and mergers. That means we can concentrate on managing our clients' assets without distraction and can afford to invest in the recruitment and development of the best talent worldwide.

Our product line-up includes fixed income, emerging market equities and debt, small cap, sector and theme funds, global and regional equities, quantitative equities, SRI, absolute return and alternative funds.

We have been managing emerging market equities since 1989 and emerging market debt since 1998 and have a reputation as pioneers in the field. In 2006 we launched local currency debt products.

Emerging economies have evolved remarkably since the Asian currency crisis of ten years ago. Their progress has driven not only emerging equity markets but also, increasingly, the emerging debt markets. In the past, emerging market economies relied heavily on external financing through hard currency debt, which has left them particularly vulnerable to sudden shifts in foreign demand. Healthier finances have allowed policymakers in the developing economies to create a virtuous circle of stronger growth, lower inflation, improved real return on equity and a more dominant role for domestic monetary policy that is less affected by changes in the supply of external capital.

- Domestic capital markets have been transformed by a combination of inflation targeting and floating exchange rates.

- The differential between the inflation rate of the JP Morgan GBI–EM index countries and that of the developed world has fallen sharply.

- Inflation targeting has reduced inflation, supported economic convergence and brought interest rates down sharply.

- Lower inflationary expectations and growing confidence in the long-term economic outlook has fostered the growth of credible financial institutions, which in turn have been able to extend yield curves.

The impact of such fundamental changes can be seen in the returns generated by emerging local bonds over the last five years.

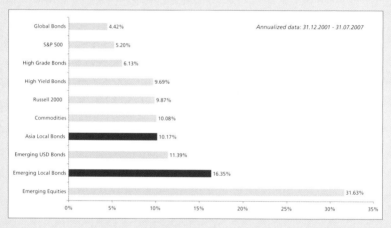

High returns from emerging local bonds in USD

Source: JP Morgan/HSBC/Bloomberg

The case for investing in local currency denominated emerging debt is therefore compelling. We think that the local emerging debt markets will ultimately develop into a mainstream asset class for long-term investors looking for elements of diversification with relatively high risk-adjusted returns.

Furthermore, we believe the investment in these regions should be considered as separate from a global bond allocation. Only by using a specialist with a long history and with a strength of resource will an investor be able to tap the full underlying potential of these growing markets.

For more information please contact:

Rod Hearn, Chief Marketing Officer
Tel: 020 7847 5000
Email: rhearn@pictet.com

Daniel Sear, Head of Business Development United Kingdom
Tel: 020 7847 5000
Email: dsear@pictet.com
Web: www.pictet.co.uk

Chapter 15
Swaps

Swaps are financial instruments that were first used in the early 1980s, when they were developed as a technique for exchanging cashflows. If you were receiving payments in dollars, then you could swap with someone else whose income was in pounds. Similarly, you could exchange your exposure to variable interest for a fixed rate.

It has proved a popular way of managing risks. As a derivative, a swap gives you exposure to an underlying asset – or stream of revenue – without incurring the expense of buying it directly. Nor does an adjustment to a position have to be made bit by bit. You can wrap it all up quickly and neatly in a single swap contract.

In the last 25 years, swaps have become a global market with a greater volume than bonds. At the end of 2006, according to the International Swaps and Derivatives Associations, the total obligations on swap contracts stood at some $235 trillion.

It is now a highly liquid market, which has a close correlation to bonds, but which offers a greater variety of products, particularly for anyone searching for longer maturities.

For you as a pension trustee, there are particular attractions in using swaps to manage the risks in your fund:

- Adjusting the allocation of assets in a portfolio, implementing negative and positive views;

- Hedging your liabilities against inflation;
- Equalising the impact of any change in interest rates by matching the duration of your assets and liabilities.

Because, like other derivatives, swaps buy you large exposure to a market for a small deposit, they are being used by some investment managers to track the market benchmark at low cost, while using the extra funds to invest in other higher performing assets.

How they work

Swaps are organised through investment banks to exchange flows of payments at set times in a defined period. Each of the two parties to the agreement is known as a 'leg'. The basic terms for swaps are laid out by ISDA, although refinements can easily be made both before and after agreement has been reached with no effect on liquidity.

The whole market operates OTC (over the counter) without any trading on exchanges at all. Prices and terms are easily available through investment banks, who often act as the counterparty themselves. In fact, they may offer to swap the entire future liabilities of a pension scheme in return for an exact flow of payments.

Dealing costs are low. Typically, there is a spread of 0.1% between bids and offers. However, the initial cost and complication of incorporating swaps into an investment strategy can be higher. Positions are also harder to unwind than simply selling a security.

Once a swap is agreed, neither party has to pay anything to each other. At the start, the two flows of payment are priced equally. However, over time the value of the vari-

NOTES

able leg will deviate, so an adjustment is made to net cash-flow. To guard against a default by either party, collateral payments are also made at regular intervals. The main risk lies in whether your counterparty will continue to exist in its present form, particularly over extended periods.

Use by pension funds

In running your funds and managing your risks, as a pension trustee you will generally use swaps in four main ways:

Interest

To neutralise the divergence in how assets and liabilities react to changes in interest rates, pension funds can exchange a floating rate for a fixed one. Swaps also give them more control over any mismatches, as, unlike bonds, they are widely available on long maturities of up to 50 years.

Inflation

For pensions whose benefits to members are tied to inflation, swaps can be appealing. Their cashflow is exchanged for earnings that are more directly linked to any rises in consumer prices, such as utilities. The counterparty, however, is often an investment bank looking to gain from its own analysis of the inflationary outlook.

Portfolio

If you want to move beyond protecting yourself from changes in interest rates and inflation, you might consider a portfolio swap. Your income is swapped for a cash flow designed specifically to meet your liabilities by an investment bank. So, instead of trying to buy securities that match your profile of payments, a single swap contract can be constructed matching your liabilities as they fall due.

Credit

Credit swaps were initially used as a technique for managing the risk of defaults or downgrades in a portfolio without having to sell the asset itself. But they have developed into instruments to increase exposure to different issuers of credit risk, such as governments and corporates.

Financial position

As with other derivatives, such as futures, swaps have become more than risk instruments. They are a highly effective means of swiftly gaining significant exposure to an asset at a low cost upfront. Returns on such leveraged investments are proportionately much higher, but so are any losses, as we saw over the summer of 2007 in the market for credit swaps related to sub-prime mortgages in the US.

Investing on this basis is speculative and lies beyond the scope of almost all pension funds. The difficulties experienced by the banking industry should not obscure the real attractions that swaps will continue to hold for trustees in managing your risks.

NOTES

Driving value from infrastructure investments

In buying and managing infrastructure investments, the ability to assess potential value and secure a business at the right price is critical. But long-term value creation lies in an active management approach applied throughout the life of the investment.

The very nature of infrastructure demands a long-term investment horizon. An outlook of 20 to 30 years is a very different proposition to, say, the three to five year timetable that typical private equity acquisitions hinge on, when efficiencies are the single driver of value.

Infrastructure businesses are capital intensive operations where the smooth delivery of essential services demands significant ongoing investment over the life of the business and commitment to meeting customer needs.

Understanding the target

In-depth knowledge of the asset is critical. Detailed due diligence at the time of acquisition should assess the company's financial structure, management team, regulatory environment and risk profile.

Having asset managers who really understand the business from an operational background means that information gained during this process not only helps determine the right bid price but is also essential for ongoing asset management including the development of business plans and strategies for business improvement.

Ongoing active management

Infrastructure assets are highly specialised businesses that require equivalent levels of expertise to manage their inherent risks – operationally, from a regulatory perspective and financially – and to create long-term value for investors.

Active, hands-on management carried out by industry experts and finance, legal and other specialists, is critical to maximising performance potential. Soon after acquisition steps must be taken to ensure the asset has the right management team and that an appropriate risk management framework is in place.

The manager can then assist business growth and development by identifying opportunities to improve operational and financial performance and providing strategic direction. Over time, further value can be created though initiatives such as divesting non-core holdings or bolt-on acquisitions.

An ongoing asset management model that takes the time to understand all relevant issues and the company's culture prior to investment, will help reduce initial risk. Coupled with strong sector expertise, this model can be very effective in achieving the goal of creating sustainable value over the long-term.

Case study: Thames Water

All of these considerations were evident in the acquisition of Thames Water in December 2006, and in managing the investment over the past year.

On behalf of the Kemble Water Consortium, Macquarie dedicated more than 40 people to the six-month bid process. Fully understanding the business and accurately assessing its risks were fundamental to succeeding in the bid.

When the acquisition completed in December 2006, the people responsible for developing the bid's investment case were now responsible for delivering it. Key management positions were replaced immediately and a 10 person strong transition team worked alongside management to create and install a business plan focussed on the core operations and delivering on the regulatory contract.

With the transition complete, Macquarie's asset management team continues to actively manage the investment. They bring significant industry, regulatory and financial expertise to the table to supplement and challenge the experience and ability in place at the company itself.

This approach, coupled with support for decisive management action, is already delivering results:

- Divestment of non-regulated businesses, enabling the business to focus on the core water and waste-water business
- Addressing leakage performance, resulting in leakage targets being met for the first time in seven years
- Implementation of strong financial governance and controls

Completion of a securitisation programme resulting in a stable long-term funding mechanism that will support the company's investment programme.

For further information on Macquarie's infrastructure asset management capabilities, contact Arthur Rakowski or Matthew Woodeson on: 020 7065 2206/2130.

www.macquarie.com/eu

MACQUARIE

A leading force in infrastructure around the globe

MACQUARIE

Macquarie has been at the forefront of infrastructure investment for over a decade.

Macquarie identified early the potential of infrastructure as a resilient, long-term asset class and our approach has been instrumental in harnessing private investment to help meet global infrastructure needs. Over a decade of experience has helped us become a global leader in infrastructure acquisition, funding and management.

With over 900 specialists worldwide we manage more than €36bn of equity in infrastructure and adjacent sectors. Our portfolio of over 100 assets in 25 countries includes water utilities, electricity and gas transmission and distribution networks, toll roads, airports, broadcast towers and social infrastructure.

Our experience sets Macquarie apart and provides a depth of expertise that is essential in managing important community assets. Macquarie-managed businesses provide water to 5 million households, distribute gas via 6.7 million connections and deliver electricity to 750,000 households.

In managing infrastructure assets we work in partnership with local management to enhance performance for the benefit of all stakeholders.

www.macquarie.com/eu

THIS IS MACQUARIE

Chapter 16
Options

Options give investors the right to buy or sell a security at a future date. It is not a right that they are obliged to exercise. If the price moves against them, they can simply allow the contract to expire.

For this chance to wait on events, investors pay an initial premium, but are not otherwise committed. If their expectations are fulfilled, their gains are open-ended. If their fears are met, then there is a floor under any losses.

For pension trustees, particularly those whose deed insists on no loss of capital, options are an effective way of protecting assets against a fall in value without giving up the prospect of higher returns. In effect, they act as an insurance policy.

Options play a role too in allowing rapid tactical adjustments to the assets allocated within a portfolio. Trustees might also encounter options in the form of 'structured products' from their fund managers. By combining bonds with equity options, they offer to guarantee a minimum return over a set period.

Calls and puts

There are two types of options which sit on either side of a contract. A 'call' is the right to buy a security by a certain date at a 'strike' price agreed now. A 'put' is the right to sell it under the same terms.

It will only be worth exercising the call if the price rises. For the owner of a put, the reverse applies: only take up your right, if the price falls.

The strike price for an option is based on the current market rate and includes a premium for the issuer. The volatility of the underlying asset will be taken into account, as well as the time span in which the option can be exercised. In going forward, the price will vary in line with the market, although if the option is illiquid changes may be more dramatic.

Options are either traded as standard contracts on a central exchange or are individually specified over the counter (OTC). On an exchange, options on assets, such as equities, bonds, commodities and interest rates, are sold as multiples on set terms. Prices are quoted continuously. As an option holder, you will not know who holds the other side of the contract, although the market is fully regulated.

On an OTC option, the contract is usually with an investment bank as the other counterparty, so more creativity can be taken in setting the terms. These agreements are unregulated.

Uses

Options allow more flexibility in managing a portfolio. At a minimum initial cost, investors can gain exposure to changes in price without having to own the underlying asset.

NOTES

Put options are widely used by pension schemes to hedge against a drop in value of a security or an index. Alternatively, if the price of an asset is expected to rise, you can purchase a call. After exercising it at the strike price, all being well, you can sell it for a profit.

As well as buying calls and puts, investors can sell them. By shorting a call, you believe the price of a security will fall. If it does, you keep the premium. If it rises, your losses are open-ended.

By selling a put, you believe the price of a security will rise. If it does, you keep the premium. If it falls, your losses are open-ended.

More complex strategies can be pursued by buying a number of options simultaneously in a way designed to exploit the risk profile of an asset or to take advantage of pricing anomalies.

In approving the use of options within a portfolio, trustees should exercise clear control over their direct and indirect use with a proper appreciation of the risk to their capital. As with other derivatives, options allow unfunded positions to be rapidly assumed, greatly magnifying the potential profits and losses.

Passive strategies – are they passé?

Janus Capital

Institutional investors today are encountering a number of challenges. Pension fund trustees must contend with the possibility of lower nominal rates of return in the equity market along with tight credit spreads in the fixed income market, rationalised risk budgets, lower participant risk tolerances and an 'underfunding conundrum'. Each plan must cope with these new realities in its own way, creating solutions unique to its individual needs and constraints. However, one thing is clear: Passive market returns earned by the massive amount of indexed assets held by today's institutional investors are unlikely to provide the returns necessary to navigate this new and more challenging environment.

Passive returns won't be enough

A pension trustee facing this dilemma has several choices: First, it could continue to allocate a significant portion to a passive index product and hope that the market produces extraordinary returns. Second, it could reset its return assumptions to reflect the new reality, in effect surrendering participants' assets to the vagaries of the market. Or, if neither of the first two choices seems attractive, it could search for ways to boost return to above market rates in an attempt to at least partially correct the underfunded status of the plan; that is, it could embark on a search for strategies capable of generating long-term alpha.

Of course, the alpha-seeking strategy chosen will depend entirely on things like the plan's initial actuarial return assumption (which drives how far "behind" it is likely to be), capital market assumptions (how well it expects markets to perform for the remainder of the decade) and overall tolerance for risk.

A renewed focus on risk

The decision to close the gap by utilising alpha-seeking strategies seems an easy one. But there's a far greater challenge: While bear markets left some plans facing deficits, it also left boards and the participants they represent far less tolerant of risk. So, while there may be a very real temptation to 'go all out' to make up for several years of underperformance (or adjust to the realities of a low nominal return environment), plans must also contend with a heightened risk sensitivity.

Plans need alpha, but they need it delivered in a reliable and consistent manner. Alternative investments, an increasingly popular option as plans search for alpha, may or may not meet both of those criteria. Most alternatives benefit from low correlations to traditional asset classes but, in reality, many of these investments come with capacity and fiduciary restraints, which may limit their use.

Hedge funds and other alternative investments: a partial solution

Despite the many benefits of including an alternatives allocation, there are obvious limitations on the extent to which they can be utilised by even the largest and most sophisticated plans. Legal restrictions, liquidity concerns, opaque disclosure and manager capacity rank among the key reasons that alternative investments – hedge funds, in particular – remain a comparatively small portion of most plan allocations.

New world, new solutions

If an increased allocation to alternatives offers only a partial solution, what is a plan sponsor to do? Enhanced index strategies are a potential solution, especially where a plan may have considerable exposure to indexed assets.

These strategies aim to deliver the predictability, discipline and low relative risk associated with passively managed products with the higher returns generally associated with active management. An enhanced index strategy seeks to outperform a passive benchmark with very low tracking error against the index. This allows a plan to participate in the market, as with a passive index strategy, and potentially realise excess returns with little additional risk which can be an attractive solution to the risk/reward challenge. However, some may find themselves under-whelmed by relatively conservative excess return goals of enhanced managers. After all, in exchange for the controlled risk profiles, most enhanced providers strive only to produce annual excess returns of 1% to 2% net of fees above the benchmark. Insubstantial? To put this in perspective, a £100 million investment will grow to £1 billion if compounded at 8% for 30 years. Adding just 1% in excess return yields £1.3 billion at the end of 30 years; while 2% excess return yields £1.7 billion – a not-so insignificant £700 million in excess return over the 30-year period. Just 1% to 2% excess return net of fees can go a surprisingly long way toward helping a plan meet long-term goals.

For more information please contact:

Tel: 020 7410 1515
Email: howard.nowell@janus.com

Alternatively, visit www.janus.com to find out more.

JANUS CAPITAL
Group

Fundamental.
Mathematical.

Two distinct approaches.
Same passion for results.

There's more than one way to generate investment returns. At Janus Capital Group we're committed to two distinct but highly complementary processes developed and enhanced over decades. The bottom-up, fundamental research driven approach of Janus and the unique risk-managed mathematical approach of INTECH.

For more information about our investment strategies, please contact Howard Nowell, UK Institutional Director on +44 (0) 207 410 1515 or email howard.nowell@janus.com.

JANUS CAPITAL
Group

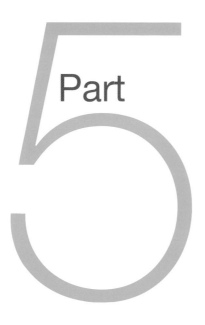

Part 5

Alternative strategies

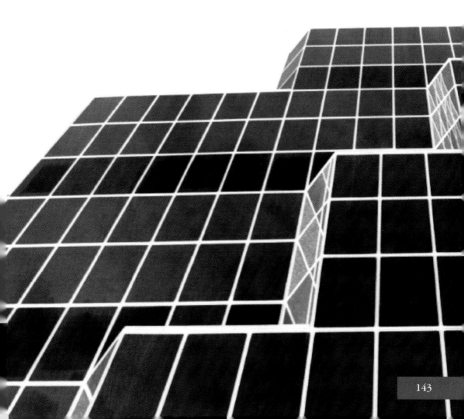

Chapter 17

Liability driven investment

The experience of the early 2000s, when pension schemes were caught between a fall in the value of their assets and a rise in the cost of their liabilities, is sparking a complete re-think of the traditional approach of managing funds. No-one wants to be exposed again to a level of investment risk that resulted in a total deficit in UK pensions that peaked at £700bn.

At the same time, the accounting treatment of future liabilities has become more precise and transparent, leaving no room for any illusions among trustees and employers that assets or contributions might somehow cover any shortfalls. In any case, the Pensions Regulator has put schemes on notice that deficits should be cleared as soon as feasible and certainly within a decade.

Liability profile

While equities have re-bounded since the low point of the bear market in 2003, pension funds remain under pressure for two main reasons: increased longevity of their members, which is hard to manage, and interest rates that have been set at historically low levels.

As pension funds have found in the last few years, the trouble is that when interest rates fall liabilities rise, because it becomes more expensive to buy annuities. The effects on the scheme tend to be disproportionate. If interest rates fall by 1%, then liabilities can rise by 10% or even 20%.

LDI (Liability Driven Investment) is a technique that has been developed to put risk firmly at the heart of investment strategy. Essentially, it is a strategic framework for mapping and managing liabilities.

LDI rejects the traditional model of asset allocation that revolves around the split between equities and bonds (or property as a proxy for fixed income). Performance is no longer measured against a market index whose constituents may or may not have any relevance to a particular scheme. Instead, each scheme has its own risk profile and its own pattern of liabilities stretching into the future.

It is a scheme's ability to meet these commitments to its members that determines its approach to risk. Any benchmark is related to that targeted rate of return. The objective is to ensure that a scheme is always in a position to meet its liabilities.

In calculating how much a fund has to pay out every year, there are a series of assumptions that have to be made. The first are fundamental. Will mortality rates rise? Will the sponsoring company fail?

Then there are two key rates that have far-reaching implications for the extent of a scheme's liabilities: interest and inflation. Essentially, LDI is about isolating these risks and nullifying their effect.

Liability matches

For proponents of LDI, the present asset structure of most funds is outmoded. The old formula of relying on a combination of equities and bonds bears little relation to variations in a scheme's liabilities. Bonds rarely correspond to peaks and troughs in cashflow. Equities are too unpredictable. The result is that schemes slip back into deficit. It is a position that no trustee wants to be in.

In fact, bonds share many of the same characteristics as liabilities. In particular, they behave in the same way when interest rates change. If the bond is inflation linked, then the other main risk for pensions can be covered. The drawback is that there is a shortage of long-dated bonds, particularly of any that are linked to inflation.

In practice, most pensions hold bonds of much shorter duration – or lifespan – than their liabilities. So, a fall in yields results in a greater increase in liabilities than in the value of bonds, so putting up the deficit again.

For mature schemes, where most of the members will be retiring in the short to medium-term, it is possible to construct an exact match of cash flows between assets and liabilities, primarily based on bonds. In the longer term, the variations are too great to lock into such a position.

However, as a trustee, you might consider matching the duration of your assets and liabilities, so they are equally sensitive to any changes in rates. Your balance between income and payments should then remain in balance. But bonds with maturities of 20, 30 or 40 years are scarce and costly.

A more liquid and flexible alternative might be to use swaps, which are contracts to exchange cash flows arranged through investment banks. Pension schemes can use them to eliminate the impact of changes in interest rates by swapping their own liabilities with someone else's on a fixed rate.

In drawing up a liability profile, you can calculate your outgoings each year and use a swap to secure a guaranteed sum to meet them. In return, you will pay the investment bank the principal at an agreed rate of interest.

If rates subsequently rise, the extra charges can be offset against the fall in the value of your liabilities. Likewise if rates fall, the increase in your liabilities will be balanced by the fall in what you pay in interest. Either way, your liabilities remain the same.

Similarly, for the many schemes that link their benefits to inflation, a swap can be set up that automatically links their liabilities to price changes.

Pooled funds

The cost and complexity of creating an individual portfolio of swaps can be high, but smaller schemes can still match their liabilities by using pooled funds. Operating on a unitised basis, these are an easier and less expensive ways of investing in derivatives against a liability benchmark.

Best returns, least risk

Creating a match for future liabilities might offer trustees peace of mind, but it is based on a forecast at a point in time. If any assumptions about risk prove to be wrong, then a scheme could find itself caught short with little room for manoeuvre. Or you could find yourself locked

NOTES

NOTES

into a position where you fail to gain from any upturn in the market and your deficit becomes permanent. Unlike equities or bonds, swaps take time to unwind.

In practice, LDI is a discipline that takes a fresh look at controlling the main risks in a scheme. Once these are isolated and covered, you should be in a position to consider a more innovative use for your remaining assets. Many funds, for instance, invest in equity options, which offer unlimited upside on a security, but put a floor under any losses.

There are no set answers. LDI is a technique for establishing the optimal balance of risk and reward in a scheme without reference to any pre-exisiting benchmark. For some, it might mean a target of outperforming bonds by 2%. For others, the figures could be as high as 6%.

In adopting LDI as an investment strategy, it is down to the trustees to gauge their own particular exposure to risk and to set an appropriate level of return. Even if a scheme is fully funded on a realistic set of assumptions, then it still usually makes sense to build a cushion against any changes, such as greater life expectancy.

Socially responsible investment

Henry Boucher

Pension funds are required by law to consider social, ethical and environmental matters in their investment decisions and, with a time horizon stretching over decades, there is a clear case for taking such a wide range of factors into account in investment decisions.

Socially Responsible Investment (SRI) has its roots in the ethical investment movement that can be traced back to the Methodists and Quakers who wished to avoid investing their money in arms, alcohol, gambling and tobacco. Today the motives for investing in a socially responsible way vary enormously but the potential impact of global warming, the social pressures of globalisation and corporate accounting scandals have acted as catalysts for a more responsible approach to investment. These issues represent the three main strands of SRI, environmental, social and governance factors (sometimes referred to as ESG).

When trustees think about socially responsible investment the first obstacle is typically confusion over the terminology used:

- SRI is an umbrella term for all investment approaches that take into account additional non-financial criteria.

- The sustainable investment approach makes investments in companies that not only offer good financial returns but also conduct themselves in a socially and environmentally responsible way. It is based on the concept of sustainable development defined in 1987 by the United Nations World Commission on Environment and Development. Sustainable 'theme' funds invest in certain industries that are regarded as being especially sustainable or in themes that have a high relevance to sustainable development, like renewable energy.

- Ethical investing is based on religious, moral and other high conviction criteria. It works by excluding specific sectors or industries such as tobacco, alcohol, gambling, armaments, pornography etc., or companies engaged in business practices such as animal testing, causing avoidable environmental damage and paying exploitative wages in developing countries. This approach is quite widely adopted by charities.

- Governance seeks to encourage accountability between company shareholders, the board of directors and other stakeholders. It is manifested in exercising voting rights at company meetings and 'engagement' in dialogue with the company, often in cooperation with other shareholders, with a view to prompting changes in corporate behaviour.

In excluding some potential investments, ethical investing is sometimes labelled as a negative screening approach. Sustainable investment combines negative screening with a more positive approach, screening investments in order to identify those with ethical business practices that promote desirable goals such as sustainable development.

There is one very common prejudice against SRI: it might be good for your conscience but it is thought to be bad for your pocket – there must be some cost for being good in a world in which 'there is no such thing as a free lunch'. Perhaps that might be the case if environmentally and socially sound corporate behaviour and long-term economic success were two totally independent issues but, in real life, the more efficient use of environmental and human resources and efficient risk management are prerequisites. And there is a lot of proof around that it is not bad for your pocket: one example is the US Domini 400 Social Index which has outperformed its conventional peer, the S&P 500 Index, since inception in May 1990 by, on average, 0.64% per year (to 31st December 2006).

For many pension funds this value added alone could neutralise the costs of their asset management. A study by the UK Environment Agency concluded that there is strong evidence that where a company has sound environmental governance policies, practices and performance this is likely to result in improved financial performance – "differences in performance between leaders and laggards being quite marked."

Beyond the basic argument for SRI, investors are also recognising that many of the investments in sustainable 'themes' have very attractive growth rates, for instance the manufacturers of wind power generators are seeing growth rates of over 25% p.a.

Many companies have realised that an integration of environmental and social policies into their business – done properly – promises a real economic advantage. For instance, avoiding waste leads to lower waste disposal costs. Fair conduct towards employees and other stakeholders pays off – contented employees are likely to be harder working and more motivated, happy suppliers are more reliable and satisfied customers are more loyal. This logic might seem a little simplistic but nobody has disproved it. Sustainable investment is not about tree-hugging, it is an investment style that not only asks how high profits are but also where the profits come from, how in a very broad sense they are achieved and how sustainable they will be in the future.

For more information please contact:

Tel: 020 7038 7000
Email: henry.boucher@sarasin.co.uk

Alternatively, visit www.sarasin.co.uk to find out more.

SARASIN
CHISWELL

NOTES

Chapter 18
Multi-asset investing

Multi-asset class investing is another strategy that questions the implicit assumptions on which pension funds in the UK have worked. It is an all-weather approach that proposes schemes should divide their portfolio into five asset classes that do not react to changes in market conditions in the same way.

In the US, it is a widely accepted formula for higher returns and proper diversification. Alongside conventional assets such as listed equities and commercial property, funds regularly devote 20% of their assets to private equity and 20% to hedge funds. The returns on bonds are generally considered to be too low, so are only held as a short-term contingency. The pioneer of this strategy, the endowment fund at Yale University, has posted annual returns of 16% over 20 years.

In the UK, MAC is slowly starting to enter the mainstream. A number of multi-asset funds are now offering a broad mix of equities, commodities, hedge funds and property not just in the UK, but on a global basis. The appeal of spreading risks across a number of assets and territories means that these funds can act as a one-stop investment shop.

However, as Guy Fraser-Sampson set out in his groundbreaking book last year, *Multi Asset Class Investment Strategy*, Wiley, MAC has more far-reaching consequences for trustees. In fact, he argues that if it had been properly adopted, pension schemes need never have found themselves with such heavy deficits in the first place.

A new mindset

"Which of us," asks Fraser-Sampson, "when asked to look after money with the heavy responsibility of a trustee would elect to put all our eggs in one basket rather than spread our investment activities over a number of different investment classes? Yet this is exactly what trustees around the world have done, and the damage that their actions have caused is plain to see."

Yet if investment strategy is such an apparent matter of commonsense, why have trustees and their investment consultants been so slow to switch from the traditional split between bonds and equities?

The answer lies in how you choose to view the performance of assets. For MAC to work, you have to break free from the annual benchmarks against which pensions have generally judged themselves.

Instead, like LDI, trustees want to gain a complete view of their commitments to their members and to set themselves a target rate of return in relation to the needs of their own particular scheme, rather than anyone else's. How the fund then performs quarter by quarter, year by year is less important than whether it reaches its eventual destination.

For trustees, that brings two considerations into play that benchmarks would normally rule out. First, returns in private markets tend to be higher than in public markets, even though they are harder to measure. Second, liquidity

THE PENSION TRUSTEE'S INVESTMENT GUIDE

within a horizon of two to three years matters, but afterwards becomes too costly.

Once trustees accept these changed parameters, they can start to put private equity, hedge funds and commodities on the same footing as conventional assets. Indeed, they will stop thinking them about as 'alternative' assets at all. Private equity and hedge funds are as different from each other as listed equities and bonds.

If the UK is to follow US practice, it will mean that instead of making a nominal allocation of 1% to alternative assets, a much larger commitment of 10% to 20% is made to each. Proper resources can then be devoted to making the best decisions for each investment class.

For private equity, in particular, it takes time to invest an allocation fully but by making a series of commitments over a number of years, its inherent risk as an asset is significantly reduced. Some investments will fail, but others will do much better than expected.

For a MAC scheme as a whole, the different way in which each of these assets reacts to changing economic circumstances and market conditions, means that it should be protected from a downturn in one any particular market. So 2002 may have been a terrible year on the stock market, as UK pension funds found to their cost, but for hedge funds it was the start of a series of bumper years.

Proper diversification allows funds to continue making compound returns each year, which ultimately represents the most effective way of meeting their total funding commitments.

Risk models

Unfortunately, according to Fraser-Sampson, MAC struggles to fit into the capital asset pricing model (CAPM) conventionally used by the pensions industry. The understanding of risk is based on how much a security is likely to vary from its overall market average based on quarterly or annual returns.

The difficulty is that an asset like private equity, which over two decades has shown the best returns of all, lies outside the parameters of CAPM and registers as too risky. The rewards only come at the end of an investment cycle of seven or eight years. In fact, for the first two or three years, losses are more likely as companies are bought and re-structured.

To compare assets more effectively, Fraser-Sampson argues that investors would be better advised to look first at 'return risk' (or whether an investment is going to meet a scheme's target rate of return) and 'capital risk' (or whether an investment could result in a loss of capital).

A genuine comparison can then be made by measuring the compound return over an entire period of an investment, not just a quarter or a year. These 'vintage' returns then give you a clear view of how each asset class is performing on a like-for-like basis. By offsetting the risks in private equity and hedge funds against other assets, trustees can put themselves in a better position to achieve better and more consistent returns.

NOTES

IS YOUR INVESTMENT STRATEGY BUILT ON SOLID GROUND?

Your investment strategy and the ability of your employer to underwrite poor investment performance is built on the foundation of your employer covenant. Here at Grant Thornton, our pensions specialists will help you protect your members' benefits with clear, independent advice. We have a track record of advice in over 250 situations and the benefit of having more staff seconded to the Pensions Regulator than any other firm. And from Bristol to Edinburgh, our national team of accredited experts are always in easy reach. So check the ground on which your scheme's employer covenant is built, by calling **Darren Mason** on **+44 (0) 20 7728 2433** to arrange a consultation.

Grant Thornton

Think beyond convention

www.grant-thornton.co.uk/pensions

Employer covenant assessment

Darren Mason, Director, Recovery & Reorganisation for Grant Thornton UK LLP

What is the financial covenant of a scheme's sponsoring employer?

Employer covenant is essentially the ability of the sponsoring and participating employers of a scheme to generate sufficient cash, when required, to fund the pension scheme.

The ability to generate cash is derived from the ability to:

- generate profits, i.e. sell things at more than the total cost of the product/service provided, as profit should ultimately over time equal cash

- borrow from financiers by pledging the companies assets in the balance sheet and/or promising to pay interest on amounts borrowed

- attract cash from investors with the promise of future growth in the value of their shareholdings or the prospect of dividends

- generate cash from selling off surplus/non core assets in the balance sheet

The ability of a company to generate profits, borrow from financiers, attract investment and sell off non-core assets to generate a profit will be different today and will change over time. Companies can increase profits, for example, by improving efficiency or increasing the volume of units they sell. Conversely, products can become obsolete or new competitors enter the market causing selling prices and profits to fall.

This is the crux of a key issue in the assessment of financial covenant. Whilst regard must be had to the financial position and performance of the business (shown in the static snapshot that is the latest profit and loss account, balance sheet and cash flow statement), an assessment must be made dynamically of the financial prospects and ability of the sponsoring employer to fund the scheme in the future. Is the sponsor going from strength to strength, or likely to experience significant competitive pressure in its chosen products and markets, with a resultant decline in cash generation and possible erosion of the assets held in the balance sheet?

For a business that is in a steady state, i.e. not undergoing a fundamental change in its products, markets and customers, and its industry sector is stable, i.e. not undergoing a period of consolidation, it should be possible to examine historic financial performance and current financial position and use this as a proxy for how the sponsor can be expected to perform in the future.

This type of review can be undertaken at relatively low but, typically c.£5 to £10k for a single legal entity with a turnover of c.£50m.

Where the sponsor is undergoing fundamental change, historic profitability and cash generation will not be a reliable proxy for the future. In these circumstances it is necessary to understand what the sponsors financial projections are, anticipating what will happen to their products, markets etc, and the reasonableness of these assumptions.

An accountant can unpick the forecasts and build a profit bridge that precisely analyses how the sponsor expects to get from £10m profit this year to £15m next year, and can challenge the assumptions as being unrealistic based on an analytical review of past experience, i.e. the assumption is product X prices will increase by 20% when an analysis of historic price increase indicates only 5% year on year price increase has been achievable. The accountant can also determine assumptions as being realistic, for example, sales volume growth of 15% being predicted on the opening new outlets against historic sales volumes in the first year of historic new store openings etc.

There is, however, a deeper insight to be gained into the financial prospects of the sponsor by carrying out this assessment together with a dedicated industry or sector specialist. They will have a much deeper understanding of the market and be able to substantiate price increases in excess of historic experience. For example by understanding that there has been a period of consolidation and, as there is under-capacity in the market, prices will be pushed up beyond historic highs. This is the principal reason Grant Thornton employs a wide variety of non-accountants that are genuine dedicated industry specialists.

Regard must also be had to the latest balance sheet information about the assets and liabilities of the business and the current level of pledges granted over the balance sheet assets and associated borrowing. An assessment can then be made of the ability of the company to pledge further assets and borrow more by reference to available assets to pledge, industry norms and bank lending criteria for borrowings relative to total assets and earnings. In this way we can understand the 'debt capacity' of the sponsor.

An assessment should also be made of the likely return to the pension scheme in a disaster insolvency scenario. This involves restating the assets to reflect break up values and restating liabilities to reflect those that crystallise on insolvency, the pension scheme full buyout deficit is one such example. It is then possible to estimate if a scheme with a full buyout deficit of £50m would recover £50m or £5m on insolvency of the sponsoring employer.

This is important because if the scheme would only recover £5m on insolvency it has much greater reliance on the ability of the sponsor to generate profits in future to fund the scheme, than if it would recover substantially all the £50m on insolvency.

The review of the balance sheet may also highlight surplus assets that might be disposed of to realise cash or be used as supporting security for a guarantee.

An understanding should then have been reached of:

- the ability going forward of the sponsor to generate cash from trading and operations;
- the sponsor's ability to borrow more, either by granting further pledges over its business or due to the strength of its earnings stream.

The employer covenant assessment might be part of a Scheme Specific Funding valuation. As part of a Scheme Specific Funding valuation the schemes actuary will have most likely prepared the valuation reflecting different levels of return on investment to illustrate the impact of investment returns varying from those anticipated. For example, a 0.5% fall in the investment return increasing the deficit by £20m.

As trustees are directed by the Code of Practice, with a covenant assessment, it is possible to determine the ability of the sponsor to cope with an additional requirement to fund £20m and underwrite the effects of adverse investment returns. Could it borrow more over five or 10 years? Is it generating sufficient profits? If not the trustees might then seek some form of guarantee from the sponsor to give the scheme greater certainty that the liability will be met and/or investigate hedging or liability driven investments etc, if they have not already done so, and balance investment strategy and funding levels with the employers covenant.

The other obvious area is in determining how quickly a sponsoring employer can reasonably afford to eliminate the deficit and fixing a recovery plan length.

It is important to mention that when carrying out the assessment of financial covenant we are examining the ability of those legally liable to contribute to the scheme. Often the sponsoring and participating employer (the entities directly legally liable to contribute to the scheme) will be part of a much larger legal entity group. In these circumstances the wider group may be willing to contribute to funding the scheme but would not be legally liable to do so until they provide a form of guarantee. Trustees should be wary about placing reliance on companies other than the sponsoring and participating employer in the absence of a form of guarantee.

People would be forgiven for thinking however that when a 'guarantee' is obtained, payment is assured. This is not the case as guarantees take many forms including, contingent, limited, unsupported, supported, several, joint and several, and the strength of the promise to pay varies, not only due to the type of guarantee, but the financial covenant of the counterparty to the guarantee, i.e. the company or individual giving the guarantee. For example, the form of the guarantee may properly confer full liability on the guarantor but this is worthless if in substance the guarantor has no ability to pay.

A typical clearance deal could be to settle the FRS17 deficit with 50% paid immediately and the balance paid over three years. However, shorter deals are done, 100% up front, and longer, i.e. balance over 10 years. The driver here is affordability, if the business has cash to clear the deficit immediately five times over the trustees could look for an up-front deal or, conversely, much longer if the business is cash constrained. There is no point in precipitating the collapse of the business by demanding too much to soon, or giving unnecessary latitude to default and never repay the deficit.

In the context of the Multi-employer Withdrawal Regulations, where it is proposed to give a guarantee to prevent the s75 debt crystallising on the exiting employer, the covenant assessment can determine whether the guarantee gives greater certainty that the full buyout liabilities will be met to satisfy the requirements of the multi-employer regulations. The work involved here is two-fold looking at the form of the guarantee and the ability of the company granting the guarantee to pay.

A covenant assessment can also justify scheme amendments, such as closing to future accrual on the grounds that the sponsor cannot afford to eliminate the deficit and meet ongoing service costs.

Employer covenant assessment is an integral part of setting and balancing appropriate investment strategy and funding levels and managing overall scheme risk.

For more information please contact:

Darren Mason
Director, Recovery & Reorganisation
Grant Thornton UK LLP
Grant Thornton House
Melton Street
London NW1 2EP
Tel/Fax: +44 (0) 870 9912433
Email: Darren.Mason@gtuk.com

Alternatively, visit www.grant-thornton.co.uk/pensions to find out more.

Chapter 19
Portable alpha

Portable alpha is an innovative technique for separating the returns in a portfolio to give you exposure to market benchmarks at minimal cost, while at the same time allowing you to gain from the superior performance of more specialised, less liquid assets, such as hedge funds.

Typically, it involves the use of derivatives to create a structure that isolates, captures and transfers the extra returns from investments that consistently outperform the market. Because derivatives only require a small down payment, you can cover your core benchmark with swaps or futures, then use – or leverage – the remaining funds to invest in other assets. In theory at least, it represents a formula for consistently outperforming efficient financial markets.

The particular attraction for trustees is that they can access sources of higher yield without exposing themselves directly to the underlying risks, giving them scope to pursue a much wider range of investments and strategies.

The downsides are that derivatives, such as futures and swaps, carry their own trading and capital risks and you have to be clear about how far you want to leverage your portfolio. You also want to be sure that you can genuinely find sources of ongoing higher returns that are not too closely related to how the core holdings in your portfolio perform.

Beta and alpha

Portable alpha draws a distinction between two types of return: beta and alpha. Beta represents the market return on an asset, benchmark or index managed on a passive basis. Alpha is the extra value added (or lost) by the skill of an investor taking positions in the market. The challenge is to find a source that always performs above beta, which over the last 20 years is calculated to have shown an annual return of between 5% and 7%.

Markets for equities and bonds are so liquid and efficient that it would be surprising to find an investor who always beats the index. Alpha is more likely to be found in more specialised markets where trading knowledge counts for more.

Hedge funds are often a source. They use a full range of trading investment techniques to profit from both rising and falling markets. But finding the right fund is usually difficult and costly. The alternative is to use a fund of funds, which can be set up against a target rate of return and against a specified level of risk.

Alpha transfer

Once alpha is found, a structure is designed to bring the returns together with beta. The first step in constructing a portfolio is to establish a scheme's target return and match it through a futures or swap contract.

On a small initial payment, the full return from an index can be gained. Some of the remaining cash in the fund will be held as collateral against the derivative. The rest can be invested in other higher yielding assets.

NOTES

But to isolate the alpha returns, an investor typically will take a long (or positive) position in an asset, such as an emerging market fund, but also go short (negative), using an instrument like an index future. In that way, any risk specific to the market can be eliminated. The yield on the net difference between the long and short positions then represents pure alpha which can be added to the returns on the beta portfolio.

Artemis Investment Management Limited

Established in 1997, Artemis is a dedicated investment management house that employs fund managers with proven track records who are passionate about investing. We focus solely on high performance active equity management and have consistently delivered returns ahead of the benchmark across all our strategies.

Artemis is a privately owned company employing 104 staff based at offices in Edinburgh and London. Assets currently total over £16bn, of which institutional assets account for over £6bn.

The strength of Artemis lies in the structure of our organisation and focus of our fund managers. As equity owners of the business and investors in our own funds our managers' interests are directly aligned with those of our clients.

The overriding philosophy that drives our fund managers is the belief that their primary aim is to beat the markets. We believe that whatever the markets are doing there will be opportunities to exploit. Fund managers are not restricted to a particular house style or process.

We offer a breadth of high performance pooled and segregated strategies for the institutional market including; UK, European and Global equities. Each of our strategies have achieved returns in excess of the benchmark in each calendar year and since inception. This demonstrates that our experienced team and robust process can consistently add value over the long term and across all market conditions.

For further information please contact Elaine Gordon or Benita Kaur at:

Artemis Investment Management Limited
Cassini House
57 St James's Street
London SW1A 1LD

Tel: 020 7399 6217
Fax: 020 7399 6497
Email: institutionalteam@artemisfunds.com
Website: www.artemisonline.co.uk

ARTEMIS
The PROFIT Hunter

Chapter 20
Pooling

In investment, scale brings advantages. You pay less for managing and running your fund. You can afford more professional advice. You gain access to a wider range of more specialised investment opportunities. You can diversify your risks by widening your exposure to different assets and territories.

Operating on their own, smaller pension funds have less choice and more expense. So it can make sense to combine their resources with others in the same position.

Pooled funds or vehicles are a way of bringing funds together under a common structure. While you will be one voice in setting investment strategy, you should be better placed to improve your balance of risk and reward.

This logic works just as well for corporations, who have been finding new uses for pooled vehicles. In particular, they are looking at how they can combine all their assets in different European countries within a single structure.

In practice, pooled vehicles are most frequently used by pension schemes:

- for index tracking and for deposits in the money markets (with the aim of keeping costs to a minimum)

- for investments in private equity, hedge funds and commercial property.

These pooled vehicles can take a number of different forms. Some are directly authorised by the Financial Services Authority. Others are unregulated, although still legal entities. Others operate on a virtual basis, where IT systems treat assets as if they were commonly held. The basis on which these vehicles actually operate has significant legal and fiscal implications for pension schemes.

Common investment funds

CIFs enable schemes to bring together assets under a single manager. The proviso is that the share of each participant must remain distinct. If the vehicle becomes 'collective' in the eyes of the FSA, then it will become subject to significant extra regulation. A formal deed is usually required to set up a CIF and approval has to be gained from Revenue & Customs.

European pooling

For companies with operations in different European countries, asset pooling is starting to become possible as an alternative to running a scheme in each country. In Luxembourg, the Netherlands, Ireland and the UK, asset vehicles have been created that are tax transparent, which means that indirect cross-border investments can be made without jeopardising the advantageous tax allowances that can be claimed in their home markets. Liabilities, however, remain resolutely national in character, so European pensions are still a long way off.

NOTES

Unit trusts and investment companies

Two types of collective investment scheme require specific authorisation by the FSA: unit trusts and OEICs (Open-Ended Investment Companies). In return for extra supervision, these schemes can be promoted to the public at large without restriction.

If they are unauthorised, as is the case when raising funds for private equity, there are restrictions on who can invest. Pension funds will have to confirm to the FSA that they are professional investors.

Unit trusts do not have fixed share capital. They are open-ended. New units are issued in response to demand. The fund's value is calculated every day and divided by the total number of units to give a buy and sell price for each unit.

Many different investment strategies are pursued by unit trusts, so pension funds have a wide choice over which ones best suit their own criteria. An initial charge is usually made on the original investment with a regular deduction for management. Stamp duty at 0.5% is also paid on any transactions.

OEICs are a corporate version of unit trusts. Essentially they are investment companies with variable capital that can be marketed throughout the EU. Many act as umbrella companies or as a fund of funds.

Limited partnerships

In subscribing to private equity, pension funds usually participate as limited partners under the terms of the 1907 Act. The main advantage is that it makes them transparent for both capital gains and income tax.

Once an investment is realised either by flotation or trade sale, each partner is held to own a proportionate share, making them responsible for paying their own taxes, from which pension schemes are in any case exempt.

Investments are mainly in the form of loans, because capital cannot be released during the life of the partnership. As limited partners, pension schemes cannot take a direct role in managing the assets, otherwise their status of limited liability will be put in jeopardy.

Appendices

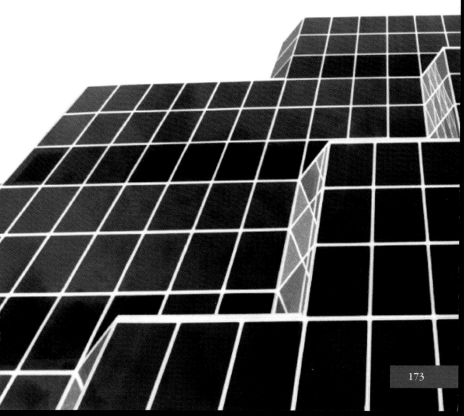

APPENDIX I
The bluffer's guide

When pensions people get together for a party, one of the party games they play is 'Definitions and Abbreviations' – there are not many who can score 100%. Set out below are some of the terms used in this Handbook, and others which you may come across in practice.

Accrual is the system under which benefits are earned year-by-year in a pension scheme. The more years you work, the more rights you accrue (or earn, perhaps). At the moment it is important in pensions at the moment because it is the basis of the argument the UK government is using in the European Court to explain that pension rights in the UK do not magically appear once you reach retirement age, but are painfully acquired (and funded for) year-by-year.

Actuary is a mathematician who by definition always gets it wrong. He estimates what he thinks the funds will earn over the next 20 years or so, what your salary will be over the next 30 years and. on the basis of these and other assumptions, calculates backwards how much money needs to be put in the kitty now. Even though he can predict the future no better than an astrologer (according to one blessed judge) he is worth every penny of his substantial fees.

Additional Voluntary Contribution was the extra contribution (not more than 15% of salary) which a member could pay into a scheme to buy extra benefits. At one time members had a right to make such contributions, but compulsory provision for AVCs disappeared after April 2006.

Administrator is an HMRC technical term to describe the person with whom the buck stops as far as they are concerned. It is your job to ensure that is not you – and is someone like the pensions manager or insurance company.

Appropriate personal pension is a personal pension which provides for an employed person a S2P benefit through a personal arrangement with a bank, building society, insurance company or unit trust. Due to the immense costs of administration charged by insurers and others – and it is not guaranteed – it is peculiarly inappropriate for most people, hence its name.

Beauty Parade is a competition you can hold where you invite potential advisers to display themselves to best advantage, indicate how little they charge, and how special is their service. It can be by post, or you can actually meet a short list. They can involve huge expense for the contestants, and are surprisingly time-consuming and exhausting to judge. You should not normally kiss the winner.

Contracting-in is the opposite of contracting-out.

Contracting-out is a system under which a company pension scheme provides benefits equivalent to one of the state pensions (the State Second Pensions – S2P (formerly the State Earnings-Related Pension Scheme – SERPS) in exchange for the employer and employee enjoying reduced National Insurance contributions. In recent years, the government offered a bribe (incentive) to persuade

NOTES

people to contract-out and anticipated the cost would be about £750m – it actually cost around £8bn, say 2p on the income tax.

Corporate Trustee is simply a trustee who is a limited company, rather than an individual.

Customer Agreement is an agreement between the trustees and the investment managers, which is required by law. Although it must state certain terms, the content of those terms is open to negotiation. Most customer agreements are very user-unfriendly.

Deferred Pensioners are people who have left the company usually to go and get a better, higher-paid job with a competitor. You may feel that they have forfeited your sympathy, but they are nonetheless beneficiaries under the scheme, and you must treat them in the same manner as you treat other beneficiaries.

Derivatives are so-called investments which are one stage removed from reality. For example, instead of buying a share in *Marks and Spencer*, you might buy *the right to buy a share in Marks and Spencer in three months time at a price fixed now* and hope that the price will rise in the meantime. If the price falls you will still have to buy the share at a loss, with money you might not have at the time. For most pension funds they are not suitable, unless used in conjunction with some other strategy, such as the intention to buy an investment overseas. Take great care and special advice. Derivatives include Swaps, Futures and Options – they are not explained because you should normally keep away from them.

Independent trustees are trustees who are not connected with the employer or the fund's advisers. They are increasingly common these days to help trustees avoid any pressures arising from conflicts of interest.

Personal pension is a pension which operates like a money box for an individual. He or she saves money each month and hopes that when retirement is reached there will be enough to buy a reasonable pension after the investment management charges, dealing fees, commission expenses, marketing overheads and administration costs have been paid, and that the Stock Market will not have collapsed three days before retirement. It can be useful, however, for young, mobile employees.

Preservation is a law which states that you do not forfeit your pension rights just because you leave the employer sometime before retirement. It is not a perfect law, but it is very much better than it used to be, and is getting better all the time. It is explained in Chapter 17.

Protected rights are the rights which, in a contracted-out money purchase scheme, replace the rights you would have earned under SERPS. Since they are money-purchase, you have no idea what they are until retirement, so that they are not in fact protected at all.

S2P is the State Second Pension which was introduced in 2002 to replace over time the State Earnings Related Pensions (SERPS). It is a flat-rate pension which gives benefits to people who are earning under £11,000 as though they had been earning that amount. Common sense dictates that since it is a flat rate pension it will eventually be merged with the Basic State Pension. It can be provided by the state (in which case the individual is contracted-in) or by a company scheme (which is contracted-out) or through a personal pension, if you are in employment (in which case it is called an appropriate personal pension).

NOTES

SERPS was the State Earnings Related Pension Scheme, a second state pension introduced by Barbara Castle in 1978.

Soft commission is so called because trustees who are soft-hearted allow fund managers to enjoy what is in effect Christmas twice-a-year. It allows investment managers to use stockbrokers to buy and sell your shares at a high commission rate so that the stockbrokers can buy them gifts (not normally cheapies, like silk stockings and champagne, but really expensive ones like Reuters screens). Don't allow it without good cause. The Myners review published by the Treasury in March 2001 recommended the abolition of soft commission arrangements.

Split fund is an arrangement which means that you divide the assets of your scheme between different fund managers and watch them compete. Some schemes have up to a dozen fund managers, but even for the smaller schemes a couple is not a bad idea.

Survivors is the modern term for 'widows and widowers'; it is shorter and discrimination-free.

Abbreviations

APSS (part of HMRC).

AVC Additional Voluntary Contribution (see Definitions).

COMPS, CIMPS, COSRS, CISRS etc Contracted-out Money Purchase Schemes, Contracted-in Money Purchase Schemes, Contracted-out Salary Related Schemes, Contracted-in Salary Related Schemes.

DWP The Department of Work and Pensions, which governs contracting-out, pensions policy and state pensions.

GMP Guaranteed Minimum Pension being the replacement (by the company scheme) for the state second tier pension. Nowadays it may not be guaranteed or provide a minimum.

HMRC Her Majesty's Revenue and Customs.

IRNICO Inland Revenue National Insurance Contributions Office.

ISDA The International Swaps and Derivatives Association.

PPF The Pension Protection Fund uses your money to protect other people's pensions. How long it will survive in its present form is uncertain.

TPAS The Pensions Advisory Service.

TPR The Pensions Regulator, formerly the Occupational Pensions Regulatory Authority (OPRA), formerly the Occupational Pensions Board (OPB).

APPENDIX II

The British Pensions System

Ministers, he [Sir Michael Partridge, Permanent Secretary at the Department of Social Security] said, regarded the far greater take-up of the scheme – and thus its far higher cost – as a 'success', not a matter for apology.

But he also disclosed that the cost of [contracting-out] rebates had been so high that ministers had had to transfer three benefits, including statutory maternity and sick pay, out of National Insurance and onto general taxation, in order to balance the National Insurance Fund's books. Michael Latham, Tory MP for Rutland and Melton told Sir Michael: "Any more successes [like that] and we are all ruined."

Nicholas Timmins, *The Independent*,
18 December 1990

The system

The British pensions system appeals particularly to people who like to do the Times crossword puzzle. It is one of the most complicated and over-regulated in the world and there are relatively few who fully understand all its implications. In brief, it works as follows:

- Everyone who has a job, including the self-employed, and earns over around £5,000pa is entitled to a basic state pension, provided sufficient contributions have been paid over the years.

- Also, an *additional state pension* (also known as S2P, the state second pension, and formerly organised as SERPS – the State Earnings Related Pension) is payable to people who have been paying extra contributions since 1978. This is payable either by the state (when it is said to be contracted-in) or by a company pension scheme (when it is said to be contracted-out) or by a personal pension scheme (when it is said to be appropriate).

- In addition, around 10 million people are earning rights under a company or *occupational pension*. The rules vary tremendously from scheme to scheme, but HMRC set down the maximum amount of pension rights (around £1.5m worth in a lifetime, say a pension of around £70,000) and no more than £215,000 contributions in any one year). For most people, that is not an issue, but the rules that control remain even more complex than they were before the great reform of the Finance Act 2004.

- Some people have decided not to join their company or workplace scheme. They can do nothing – or make contributions to a *personal pension scheme*. A personal pension is the only kind of pension which the self-employed can enjoy. A personal pension can only be money purchase, not final salary.

NOTES

State pension credit

The state pension credit is in two parts: the guarantee credit and the savings credit. The guarantee credit is a form of means-tested income support for the over-60s who are on low income and work fewer than 16 hours a week. Lower benefits are paid where there are savings of over £6,000. The savings credit is intended to reward anyone who has made their own provision for retirement. It is paid from age 65, and pays an allowance of 60p per £1 of income between around £80 and £110. No savings credit is paid where income exceeds around £150. The joint complexity of these two benefits (a payment if you have not saved, and a payment if you have) is under review and it may be that all the state pension arrangements will be ditched in favour of a simple single pension paid to everyone over a certain age.

HMRC rules

HMRC lays down the rules which decide whether pension funds are eligible for tax relief. Nowadays their jurisdiction is diminishing slightly as they have foregone control of unapproved unfunded schemes which provide pensions for top-earners; but in most cases they are concerned to police schemes to ensure that the benefits they pay are within bounds and that they do not provide benefits worth over around £1.5m in total without paying extra tax.

It is not clear whether the skies would fall in if HMRC were abolished and replaced by some simple rules (as in other countries). There were around eight different tax systems that could apply to pensions, depending on when the member joined, when the scheme was set up, and what kind of scheme it is. Now there is only one, but more pages of law than ever before.

Self-administered and insured

All company pension schemes in the UK are strictly speaking self-administered, ie managed by trustees. But schemes which have delegated all the investment and administration to insurance companies are said to be 'insured'.

For trustees, there may be problems with insured schemes. Firstly, it is sometimes very difficult to work out what the management and investment expenses are (usually higher than self-administered schemes for all but the smallest funds). Secondly, the actuary sometimes has a conflict of interest between acting for you and acting for his employer (the insurance company), and may be tempted to suggest higher contribution rates for example than might be strictly necessary (in order to raise fees) or lower amounts than might be prudent (in order to get business). Thirdly, the contracts imposed by insurers (if you ever get a chance to see them) can be rather one-sided, in their favour, with unacceptable penalty clauses for early discontinuance – which is why almost all the larger pension schemes tend to go self-administered as soon as they are old enough.

Money purchase and final salary

A final salary (defined benefit) scheme is one of the great antidotes to the effect of inflation on pensioners, although it is not perfect. It promises benefits related to the salary at the date of leaving, usually according to some formula related to the number of years you have worked with the company. One example is to promise a pension of 1/60th

NOTES

of final salary for each year you work with the company. If you work for 40 years, you will get 40/60ths, ie 2/3rds. With luck there may be some element of inflation protection once the pension starts in payment. (The Americans call this kind of scheme 'benefits-related'.)

A money purchase (defined contribution) scheme doesn't promise anything at all. It establishes a kind of piggybank into which your contributions and those of the employer (if any) are paid. The money is invested – and at the end of the day whatever is available is gambled with an insurance company. Your bet is that you will live a long time, and the premium or wager will pay off. The insurance company hopes on the other hand you will die soon, so it can make a profit. The value of the pension depends not on your salary at retirement, but on what the accumulated pot will buy at the time – and the value of the pot may be affected by changes in the value of the shares or other assets at the date you retire.

Unfunded schemes

The point of a funded scheme is that if the employer does not meet his promise for any reason (eg bankruptcy) there will be money available to meet the promise. HMRC rules now make it tax inefficient (with some exceptions) to pre-fund pension rights in excess of broadly £70,000pa, so there is no security for those with higher pensions.

AVCs

As very few people actually spend 40 years with one company, very few people actually accrue full pension benefits (for why not, see Chapter 17). They were therefore allowed to make additional contributions (within limits – 15% of their salary) to their scheme. These were known as Additional Voluntary Contributions, for obvious reasons. Because of changes to the tax rules, individuals can now gain pension rights of up to £215,000 a year, and there are no limits as to how many pension schemes they can contribute to, so it is now up to schemes themselves whether they will allow you to make AVCs.

APPENDIX III

Pensions by numbers

What tax relief is there on pensions?

In fact pensions cost the state very little indeed in terms of lost tax; pension arrangements are largely fiscally neutral, rather than fiscally privileged because although there is tax relief on the contributions made and the build up of investments, tax is paid on the benefits. There is, however, an advantage in that some of the pension can be taken as a tax-free lump sum, and that sometimes the income tax paid on the pension is lower than the tax that would have been paid on the salary.

The Treasury considers that the annual tax relief given amounts to £16bn; most normal people consider the opposite is true – that the pensions movement probably contribute to the Exchequer around £5bn a year on balance, ie it is tax inefficient for companies to pay into funded arrangements than simply to pay a lower salary in retirement.

Can I live on the basic state pension?

Since 1948, single person, pa, £

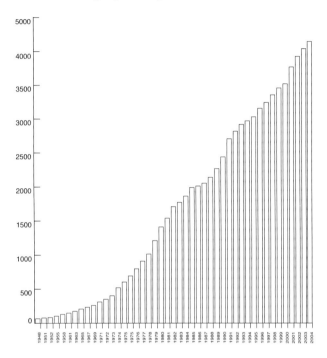

1948	£67.60	1984	£1,861.60
1951	£78.00	1985	£1,991.60
1952	£84.50	1986	£2,012.40
1955	£104.00	1987	£2,054.00
1958	£130.00	1988	£2,139.80
1961	£149.50	1989	£2,267.20
1963	£175.50	1990	£2,438.80
1965	£208.00	1991	£2,704.00
1967	£234.00	1992	£2,815.00
1969	£260.00	1993	£2,917.20
1971	£312.00	1994	£2,995.20
1972	£351.00	1994	£3,060.20
1973	£403.00	1996	£3,179.80
1974	£520.00	1997	£3,247.40
1975	£603.20	1998	£3,364.40
1975	£691.60	1999	£3,471.00
1976	£795.60	2000	£3,510.00
1977	£910.00	2001	£3,770.00
1978	£1,014.00	2002	£3,926.00
1979	£1,211.60	2003	£4,027.40
1980	£1,411.80	2004	£4,139.20
1981	£1,539.20	2005	£4,226.60
1982	£1,708.20	2006	£4,381.00
1983	£1,770.60		

What will pensions cost the country?

The government is concerned about the future cost of state pensions, which is why it encourages private pension provision with tax breaks. Recent estimates suggest the cost of public sector pensions might amount to £690bn in March 2005 (Watson Wyatt, February 2004); this excludes the cost of state pensions. But it is expected that state pension arrangements in the next few years will be simplified immensely, and paid later in life at a higher rate than presently. Current spending suggests it will involve around 6.3% of GDP by 2050, up from 5.9% of GDP at present (around £65bn pa). This is around half the average for other EU Member States.

How important is grey power?

The UK has about 11 million people over state pension age, about 20% of the population. Adding all those over the age of 55, and taking into account the fact that older people vote much more often then younger people, some observers suggest that those over 55 have around 80% of the voting power in the UK.

How long will I live?

The life expectancy for a man aged 65 was about 11 years in 1950; by 2050 it is expected to be about 28 years.

How important are workplace pensions?

In 1979 around 30% of single pensioners enjoyed an occupational pension on average of £40 a week; by 2001, around 50% of single pensioners enjoyed around £80 a week from

NOTES

occupational pensions. The number of workplace pensioners is expected to fall over the coming years.

Are there enough people working to support me in my old age?

The dependency ratio (the number or people working age 20-64, compared with the number of retired people over age 65) in 1941 was around five to one; by 2050 it is expected to be about two to one.

APPENDIX IV
Bluffer's cases

One of the things that irritates many trustees is the throw-away reference made in conversation by advisers to famous law cases. Set down below are brief outlines of some of the more important cases, and ones which are referred to frequently in practice. Because three of the cases deal with the Imperial Group pension scheme, they have been given their alternative colloquial names to avoid confusion. References are given to enable further study if required. A full treatment here is not possible; there are now around a hundred cases a year in the courts, and several hundred ombudsman decisions, many emerging from company reconstructions, the interpretation of deeds or insolvency.

Investments

Scargill

Arthur Scargill, the miners' leader, was a trustee with other union members of the mineworkers' pension scheme. When the in-house fund managers produced an investment plan and sought the approval of the trustees, he objected. The plan included investments in property in the United States, and in oil shares; the union objected on the grounds that a UK fund should invest in the UK to support the UK economy, and that a coal pension fund should not support the shares of a competing fuel industry.

The judge held that the only objective which trustees should bear in mind is the financial performance of the fund; trustees should not promote their external objectives which might have an adverse impact on the fund's performance. It did not hold that social and ethical investments were inappropriate for pension funds; but where these criteria are involved trustees need to ensure that their members will not suffer. (*Cowan v Scargill, Re Mineworkers Pension Scheme Trusts [1985] Ch 270*).

Grumman

This is an American case – but very relevant to current problems. Although it is forbidden for pension funds to buy too much of its parent company's shares nowadays, it may have some shares, or shares in the predator. Should it take the best price – or help out the employer? Conventional trustee thinking should say: take the money and run. But other minds have thought that you could take into account job prospects and other matters affecting the members for whom you care.

The Department of Labor in the States (which looks after pension schemes) sued the trustees who had refused to sell the Grumman fund's shares in Grumman, the fighter aircraft manufacturer, to Lockheed which had made a juicy offer. But by the time the case came to trial, the share price was higher than ever, so the Department could not show the trustees had made a loss, and dropped the case. (*Blankenship v Boyle* (1971) 329 F Supp 1089)

Surpluses – whose money is it?

Hillsdown

When Hillsdown bought a subsidiary company from the Imperial Group, the bulk transfer payment received in respect of the members who became employed by Hillsdown did not include a share of the surplus in the Imperial fund. The judge said that in reality the surplus was 'temporary surplus funding' by the employer, and that in the particular case the members had no interest in it. For a short time it indicated that there was nothing wrong in employers claiming a return of surplus. (*Re Imperial Foods Ltd Pension Scheme* [1986] 1 WLR 717). The compliance rules (if surpluses ever return) would be a little different now, but the principle is now well established in other later cases.

Courage

The next year, in a case involving the same scheme, a different judge held, however, that surpluses could not be automatically recovered by an employer as part of a commercial transaction. There was no principle that a surplus by its nature was the employer's, even in a 'balance-of-cost' scheme, that is where the employer pays whatever contributions are deemed necessary by an actuary. This made it difficult for advisers to determine when a surplus could be recaptured by employers, and when it could not. (*Ryan v Imperial Brewing and Leisure, Re Courage Group's Pension Schemes* [1987] 1 WLR 495)

Mettoy

When the Corgi toy car company went bust, it left behind a string of debts and a large pension scheme. The scheme was so large it had around £9m surplus left after the scheme trustees had bought the appropriate benefits for all the pensioners and other members. The question was whether the liquidator of the company could also act as trustee of the fund, and pay himself (as liquidator) the surplus, which he could then pass on to the creditors of the company.

After a fair chunk of the surplus had been spent on legal fees (not just the fault of the lawyers – the judge insists on all conceivable parties (such as widows and children) being separately represented) and many years travelling through the courts, the judge simply said that he would approve a deal involving improvement of benefits and return of surplus, if it were brought to him. (*Re Mettoy Pension Scheme* [1990] Pensions Law Reports 9)

Davis v Richards and Wallington

This is another case where the employer was in liquidation. The judge said that if it had not been for the fact that the documentation was in force, the surplus in relation to the employers' contributions could be returned to the employer – and the surplus in relation to the employees' contributions would have to go to the Crown! The judgment seems deeply flawed, but it shows that there are several ways of looking at what a surplus is – or was.

Fisons

Fisons, a fertiliser and chemicals company, sold its agrochemicals subsidiary to a another company. In the time between the sale and the time when the bulk transfer payment was made in respect of the employees who had transferred, the Stock Market rose. Should the transfer value reflect that a surplus had arisen – or be based on the original deal set out in the sale and purchase agreement? In yet another rather odd judgment the Court of Appeal said that where the employees stay in the scheme while the new employer sets up a new scheme, they are entitled to a share of the surplus. The case is a worry for trustees, and they need to ensure that their lawyers have covered the position in the sale and purchase agreement. (*Stannard v Fisons Trust Ltd*)

Equal treatment

Barber

Mr Barber was made redundant at the age of 52 and his employer offered people within ten years of retirement an early retirement pension. His normal retirement age was 65, and he was therefore not within ten years – but a female colleague in the same position but whose retirement age was 60 (reflecting the state retirement age) would have been entitled to call for an early retirement pension.

The European Court of Justice held that pensions were to be regarded as pay, covered by the equal pay law of the Treaty of Rome, and Mr Barber (or rather his widow – he had died by the time the case came to court) was entitled to the benefit.

The major problem was whether the decision affected pension rights acquired by men before the date of the judgment (May 1990) – if so it would have enabled all men to have an unreduced early retirement pension, cost UK plc around £50bn, and bankrupted a number of employers. Fortunately, before any further cases went to court the matter was settled by an amendment to the Treaty of Rome, which indicated that pension rights earned before May 1990 were not covered. (*Barber v Guardian Royal Exchange Assurance Group*, Case C262/88, [1990] 2 All ER 660). This was a very famous case at the time – and the reverberations of the decision continue today in relation to the equal treatment of part-time employees, the details of which remain to be settled.

Employers and trustees

Mihlenstedt

A bank clerk in her thirties complained of illness and asked for an ill-health early retirement pension. As such a pension is very expensive to provide, the trustees could only give it with the consent of the employer. Since medical examinations failed to disclose any illness, the employer refused. The judge said that the employer's refusal had to be fair (and as though he were a trustee of the scheme) and not just based on a desire to save money for the company. In fact the company had behaved properly – but the case imposed a new obligation on employers, and made the use of employer's vetoes problematical. The case is a problem for employers, rather than trustees. (*Mihlenstedt v Barclays Bank International Ltd* [1989] Pensions Law Reports 124)

Imperial

The employer tried to squeeze surplus out of a (closed) pension scheme by saying that he would not agree to any increases in pensions-in-payment over 5% (on which he had a veto) unless the trustees and members agreed to move over to another pension scheme. The judge said that employers had to use such vetos (consents) as though they were trustees, not to force through decisions under which they could benefit. Since the company was Hanson, which had a reputation for attempting to squeeze pension funds, there was not much sympathy for the employer. But the decision raised the interesting question of what is the function of such a veto, if it is not to save the company money. (*Imperial Group Pension Trust Ltd v Imperial Tobacco Ltd*)

APPENDIX V
Addresses

Trustees can usually rely on their in-house support (if any) or their advisers to deal on a day-to-day basis with the regulators and other institutions. But there may be times when you need to get in touch direct, perhaps to check that something has been done, or to complain about the quality of service of an adviser. Set out below are some of the more useful addresses and phone numbers.

Accounts

Pensions Research Accountants Group (PRAG)
David Slade, Deloitte & Touche, Four Brindleyplace
Birmingham B1 2HZ dslade@deloitte.co.uk
(www.prag.org.uk)

Actuarial matters

In England and Wales

Institute of Actuaries
Director: Caroline Instance, Staple Inn Hall
London WC1V 7QJ
020-7632 2100
www.actuaries.org.uk

Consulting actuaries

Association of Consulting Actuaries
Warnford Court 29, Throgmorton Street
London EC2N 2AT
020-7382 4594
www.aca.org.uk

In Scotland

Faculty of Actuaries in Scotland
Mclaurin House, 18 Dublin Street
Edinburgh EH1 3PP
0131-240 1300
www.actuaries.org.uk

Consultants

Society of Pensions Consultants
John Mortimer, Secretary, St Bartholomew House
92 Fleet Street, London EC4Y 1DH
020-7353 1688
www.spc.uk.com

Consumer affairs

Complaints and remedies

TPAS The Pensions Advisory Service
Malcolm McLean, Chief Executive, 11 Belgrave Road
London SW1V 1RB
020-7630 2270
www.pensionsadvisoryservice.org.uk

NOTES

Occupational schemes

Pensions Ombudsman
Tony King, 11 Belgrave Road
London SW1V 1RB
020-7834 9144
www.pensions-ombudsman.org.uk

Personal pensions

Financial Ombudsman Service
Walter Merrick, South Quay Plaza, 183 Marsh Wall
London E14 9SR
020-7964 1000
www.financial-ombudsman.org.uk

Europe and international

The Double Century Club
David West, Aon Consulting, 15 Minories
London EC3N 1NJ
020-7767 2151
david.west@aonconsulting.co.uk

DWP International Pensions Centre
Tyneview Park, Newcastle-upon-Tyne NE98 1BA
0191-218 7777
www.thepensionservice.gov.uk

Industry

National Association of Pension Funds
Joanne Segars, Chief Executive, NIOC House
4 Victoria Street, London SW1H ONX
020-7808 1300
www.napf.co.uk

CBI Pensions Working Group
Employment Affairs Directorate, CBI
103 New Oxford Street
London WC1A 1DU
020-7379 7400
www.cbi.org.uk

Investment

UK Society of Investment Professionals
Chief Executive
90 Basinghall Street
London EC2V 5AY
020-7796 3000
www.uksip.org

Institutional Shareholders Committee
Joanne Segars, Chief Executive, NAPF
NIOC House, 4 Victoria Street
London SW1H ONX
www.napf.co.uk

NAPF Investment Committee
Joanne Segars, Chief Executive
NAPF, NIOC House, 4 Victoria Street
London SW1H ONX
www.napf.co.uk

NOTES

Investment Management Association
Richard Saunders, Chief Executive
65 Kingsway, London WC2B 6TD
020-7831 0898
www.investmentuk.org

Lawyers

Association of Pension Lawyers
Derek Sloan, Chairman, c/o PMI House
4-10 Artillery Lane, London E1 7LS
020-7247 1452
www.apl.org.uk

Personal pensions

Association of British Insurers
51 Gresham Street, London EC2V 7HQ
020-7600 3333
www.abi.org.uk

Population and demography

Government Actuary's Department
Trevor Llanwarne, Government Actuary, Finlaison House
15-17 Furnival Street, London EC4A 1AB
020-7211 2600
www.gad.gov.uk

National Statistics
1 Drummond Gate, London SW1V 2QQ
0845 601 3034
www.statistics.gov.uk

Pensions profession

Pension managers

The Pensions Management Institute
Vince Linnane, Chief Executive, PMI House
4-10 Artillery Lane, London E1 7LS
020-7247 1452
www.pensions-pmi.org.uk

Regulation and compliance

Department of Work and Pensions
Private Pensions, The Adelphi
1-11 John Adam Street, London WC2N 6HT
020-7712 2171
www.dwp.gov.uk

The Pensions Registry
PO Box 1NN
Newcastle on Tyne
NE99 1NN
0191-225 6316

The Pensions Regulator
Tony Hobman, Chief Executive
Invicta House, Trafalgar Place
Brighton BN1 4DW
01273-627600
www.thepensionsregulator.gov.uk

The Pension Protection Fund
Partha Dasgupta, Chief Executive
Knollys House, 17 Addiscombe Road
Croydon, Surrey CRO 6SR
0845-600 2541
www.pensionprotectionfund.org.uk

Financial Services Authority London

Inland Revenue (Policy)
Mark Baldwin, Inland Revenue
Room No: 1/38, 1 Parliament Street
London SW1A 2BQ
020-7417 2939
mark.baldwin@ir.gsi.gov.uk

Tax

Inland Revenue
(Savings, Pensions and Share Schemes,
Audit and Pension Schemes Services)
Yorke House, Castle Meadow Road
Nottingham NG2 1BG
0115-974 1600
www.inlandrevenue.gov.uk/pensionschemes

APPENDIX VI
Further reading

The library of books and videos on pensions is now almost without number. If you'd like to explore this fascinating subject more clearly, some of the more readable texts include:

General

The entire raw materials on pensions, trust and investment law is found in only one place in organised form: *Perspective* (www.pendragon .co.uk); it is in its main form a professional information tool, but the best. A cut down version for trustees is expected soon.

The Pensions Regulator (www.thepensionsregulator.gov.uk) has a widening range of booklets mostly in minatory mood; they are all available free on their website or by post. Current issues include *Appointing professional advisers: a guide for occupational pension scheme trustees; a guide to help their pension scheme clients comply with pensions legislation; Pension scheme trustees: a guide to help occupational pension scheme trustees understand their duties and responsibilities; A guide to appointing professional advisers; A guide for occupational pension scheme trustees; A guide to solving disputes; A guide for trustees of occupational pension schemes; Getting your audited accounts and the auditor's statement on time; A guide for occupational pension scheme trustees; A guide to audited scheme accounts; A guide for people involved with insured salary-related pension schemes; Record keeping for your pension scheme; A guide for trustees of insured occupational pension schemes.*

You probably do not need to read all of these, but it is handy to know they are around if you need them in a particular instance.

The National Association of Pension Funds (www.napf.co.uk) has a series of 'made simple' guides which are well worth browsing; they include: *Pensions act made simple; Voting made simple; Cash management made simple; Corporate bonds made simple; Equity derivatives made simple; Transaction costs made simple; Venture capital and private equity made simple.*

Periodicals

Weeklies

There are two main weeklies: *Pensions Week*, Financial Times Business, One Southwark Bridge, London SE1 9HL (020-7873 3000). Nominal subscription is £185, but you should be able to get it free, especially if you are an NAPF member. The other is *Professional Pensions* Incisive Media, 1st Floor, 2 Stephen Street, London W1T 1AN (020-7034 2600) £325 a year nominal but free if you insist.

Monthlies

There is one 'official' periodical, *Pensions World* (LexisNexis, 2 Addiscombe Road, Croydon, Surrey CR9 5AF I (020-8662 2000) £84 per annum. Content and layout is a little dry for most tastes and it is minimally sub-edited, but it does have the basic information – plus a monthly shower of leaflets and booklets, some of which are worth reading –

NOTES

and it is relatively cheap.Try the half-page summary of legal developments at the end if you cannot manage any more.

Most of the others are also designed for pensions technicians or salesmen, but *Occupational pensions* (LexisNexis, 2 Addiscombe Road, Croydon, Surrey CR9 5AF (020-8662 2000) www.irsonline.co.uk ISSN 0952-231X) designed for personnel people is usually readable. *Pensions today* is an 8-page monthly (very expensive £426 pa) but an easy idiosyncratic read www.informafinance.com (Informa Finance 30-32 Mortimer Street London W1W 7RE (020-7017 4072)). Informa also issue a monthly *Pension scheme trustee*, which is worth a look, but is a little heavy going for some tastes.

International information is available from still the best (and free) *IPE* (Investment and Pensions Europe), 320 Great Guildford Street, London SE1 OHS (020-7261 0666). *European Pensions News* is twice a month, very good, but expensive (£575) (020-8606 754) www.ftbusiness.com Financial Times Business, One Southwark Bridge, London SE1 9HL (020-7873 3000). *Global Pensions* is also published monthly (MSM International MSM International Thames House 18 Park Street London SE1 9ER (020-7378 7131); some people pay a subscription, but there is free access to their website if you register www.globalpensions.com. See also *Pensions international* (Informa Finance 30-32 Mortimer Street, London W1W 7RE (020-7017 4072)) www.informafinance.com.

Quarterlies

The only quarterly readily available is *Pensions: an international journal*, which looks at issues both of policy and detail in greater depth (Palgrave Macmillan, Brunel

Road, Houndmills, Basingstoke, Hampshire RG21 6XS, 01256 357 893).

Many of the financial pages in the daily and weekly newspapers offer very good summaries of current issues; you should keep a watching brief on them. For information on the web try www.ipe.com; www.pensionnet.com; www.pensionsworld.co.uk; and www.thepensionsite.co.uk

Law

Textbooks

There is one major textbook, written by the author, called *Pensions law and practice* (Sweet and Maxwell, 4 vols, looseleaf, £450, ISBN 0-85121-306-5). Whilst well-printed, and looking impressive on the bookshelf, it may be a little intimidating for everyday use. For the trust technician *The law of occupational pension schemes* (Nigel Inglis-Jones, Sweet & Maxwell ISBN 0-421-3580-8) is handy.

Equity and trusts

If you are fascinated by the law of trusts and their history, skip most of the conventional texts. A readable though long book, available in paperback, and much appreciated by trust lawyers, is Graham Moffat and Michael Chesterman, *Trusts law: texts and materials*, Butterworths Law, 2004, ISBN 0-4069-72664 £29.95.

The standard book is *Underhill & Hayton: Law relating to trustees*, (2002, ISBN 0-4069-38849 £315). And if you don't like this Handbook, you could try a somewhat different approach: Roger Self, *Tolley's Pension fund trustee handbook* (LexisNexis). The Pensions Regulator publishes the rather more formal *A guide for pension scheme trustees*, packaged with this book (www.thepensionsreg-ulator.gov.uk).

If you are preparing yourself for one of the certificates, there is *The guide for pension trustees*, looseleaf (NTC 01494 418605) which also includes an examination preparation pack. And for a view of the way in which these things are done in the States, look at *Understanding and managing fiduciary responsibility* (Principal Financial Group).

Law reports

You should not need to read law reports; if you are keen you can suggest your manager might take them, and your lawyer should certainly subscribe to them (Pensions Benefits Law Reports, www.pensionslaw.org) £250 pa) or available on the forthcoming trustee version of Perspective (020-7608 9000).

Tax. You need to be a Senior Wrangler to understand the tax structure of pension schemes. Most of the tax books were out of date from 2006.

Social security

You cannot be serious if you want to refer to the social security law; if you must, try *The blue volumes, volume 5* (The Law Relating to Social Security: Occupational and Personal Pensions, Corporate Document Services (DWP), ISBN 0-8412-35466, £19, looseleaf).

Statutes

The amount of raw pensions law has increased over the last 20 years from about 40 pages to about 8,500 pages. Much of it is all reproduced, more or less accurately, in

Butterworths Pensions legislation (LexisNexis, looseleaf, ISBN 0-4069-98388, £286.67). Most professionals use *Perspective*, which also lets you track the changes in the law. If you need a bit of a shock, try the www.pendragon.co.uk (the *Perspective* website, open access), which lets you scroll through all the new law that has had to be absorbed over the last few years. That scroll effect shows why the pensions system is overloaded.

The pensions system

General

There are innumerable guides to the pensions system. One of the more practical is *Pensions handbook* (Tony Reardon, Prentice Hall, 2003, ISBN 0-2736-75419, £31.99), though a little technical. The general pensions issue is looked at by, amongst very many others, *The pension challenge*, edited by Olivia Mitchell and Kent Smetters, Oxford University Press, 2004, ISBN 0-13-144603-7 £40. But the most useful source of all is the Pensions Policy Institute which is producing an increasing range of easy-to-read and on-the-point papers and discussion papers (www.pensionspolicyinstitute.org.uk).

If you would like to look at the history of pensions, there is Chris Lewin, *Pensions and insurance before 1800: a social history*, Tuckwell Press, ISBN 1-86232-2112, 2004, £25.

Company policy on pensions is explored in *A view from the top: a survey of business leaders' views on UK pension provision* (CBI, April 2004 ISBN 0-85201-597-6, £7)

Insurance Policies

There is no shortage of works on which is the best insurance contract; unfortunately none of them will tell you which will be the best policy in twenty five-years' time. Figures are published monthly in a monthly periodical *Money management.*

Jargon

The jargon of pensions is legion. You could try *Pensions terminology – a glossary for pensions schemes,* (6th ed 2002) published by the Pensions Management Institute (www.pensions-pmi.org.uk).

International

If you think it's bad in Britain, it's worth looking sometimes at what happens in the rest of the world. Always as up to date as these things can be, *International benefit guidelines annual* (Mercer Human Resources, Telford House, 14 Tothill Street, London SW1H 9NB, no longer free unfortunately). Also good value is *Employee benefits in Europe* but dating fast (Howard Foster, Sweet & Maxwell).

Accounting

The impact of FRS 17, the standard set by the accountancy profession for the disclosure of pensions obligations on the accounts of companies, has concentrated the minds of many companies on the pensions issue. It can be a technical area, and is changing very fast, but if you want to avoid being out bluffed, one of the most useful guides is *Accounts & audit of pension schemes* (Amyas Mascarenhas & Teresa Sienkiewics (Touche Ross), Butterworths, 2nd ed, ISBN 0-406-00348-3 £26.50, 240pp pb). More recent is Jo Rodger, *Accounts and audit of pension schemes*

(LexisNexis, November 2002). There is also the Pensions Regulator's guide for trustees (see above) and technical notes issued by various accountancy bodies.

Investment

Investment is the fun part of being a trustee; unfortunately there is very little recent UK material for the non-expert and there seems to be a gap in the market. There are occasional brochures from asset managers, and the NAPF publishes some 'made simple' leaflets (see above), but most of the standard guides are now very dated and have not been replaced. In relation to ethical investments, there is David Bright, *Socially responsible investment - a guide for pension funds and institutional investors* (Monitor Press, 2000) and EIRIS (Ethical Investment Research Service) operates widely in this area (www.eiris.org).

Policy

If you are interested in examining why pensions systems are so complicated you might like to look at some of the government papers on certain problems.

Mergers and acquisitions

The then Occupational Pensions Board published a series of readable reports, one of which is on what happens to pension funds on take-overs and mergers. It is now hard to find, but it foretold many of the problems we now suffer from: *Protecting pensions* (Department of Social Security, *Protecting pensions: safeguarding benefits in a changing environment*, February 1989, HMSO Cm 573, ISBN 0-10-105732-6, £8.30).

NOTES

Equal treatment

A superb analysis of the problems of equal treatment is the House of Lord's Social Services Committee *Report on the age of retirement* (HCP3 1981-2). For a beautiful discussion (literally) of the problem of rationalising the state pension age, see *Options for equality in state pension age*, (DSS, HMSO Cm 1723, ISBN 0-10-117232-X, £9.80).

Demography

There is a huge literature on 'whither pensions'; some of the more readable include *Workers versus pensions: intergenerational justice in an ageing world* (edited by Paul Johnson and others, Manchester University Press, 1989, ISBN 0-7190-3038-2, £22.50). If you want to know how pensioners feel, read the spoof *The thoughts of pensioner activist and radical granny Betty Spital*, (Christopher Meade, Penguin, 1989, ISBN 0-14-012150-1, £3.99). The Organisation for Economic Co-operation and Development has produced *Aging populations: the social policy implications* (OECD, from HMSO, 1988, ISBN 92-64-13113-2, £12 pb) which is much shorter, 90pp – by 2040 the proportion of people over 65 will have doubled.

The pensions system

If you would like to read background papers on the reform of the pension system in 1986 and later, it is all set out in what became known as The Fowler Report (in homage to the Beveridge report half-a-century before): *Reform of social security* (3 vols, Cmnd 9517, 9518, 9519, 1985, ISBN 0-10-195170-1, 0-10-195180-9, ISBN 0-10-195190-6, £3, £6,60 and £10, HMSO). A bizarre and very personal approach was set out in *Pensions and privilege: how to end the scandal, simplify taxes and widen ownership* (Philip Chappell, Centre for Policy Studies, 8 Wilfred Street,

London SW1E 6PL, 1988, ISBN 1-870-265-23-8, £5.50)
which attacked company pension schemes in rather intem-
perate language. It is interesting to read to see how some
of the ideas proposed there have now come to grief. More
recently the Pensions Commission and the Pensions Policy
Institute have both published outstanding guides to the
present system (Pensions Commission, *Pensions: challenges and choices*, www.pensionscommission.org.uk,
October 2004).

Trade unions

Unfortunately there are at present few suitable guides to
trade union practice in pensions, although the TUC
pensions department and certain leading unions such as
the EETPU and others provide an excellent service to
members. A brief and sensible guide is *The LRD guide to
pensions bargaining*, (Labour Research Department, 78
Blackfriars Road, London SE1 8HF, 1988, ISBN 0-946-898-
650, £1.25) and a more partisan view is set out in *The
essential guide to pensions: a worker's handbook*, (Sue
Ward, Pluto Press, 1988, ISBN 1-85305-093-8). Both are
ancient and not easy to find, but there seems little newer.

Social security

Social security and its impact on pensions is a minefield.
The standard guide is *Tolley's social security and state
benefits* (Jim Mathewman, annual, £24.95 ISBN 0-85459
502-3, Tottel)

State benefits

A very useful and understandable guide is *Your Guide
to Pensions 2005 Planning ahead to boost retirement
income*, Sue Ward, ISBN: 086242397X, 184pp September
2004 and *Your rights* 2004-2005, *A guide to money bene-*

fits for older people Sally West, ISBN: 0862423937, 176pp, April 2004, £4.99

Communication

One of the undervalued areas of pensions, marketing your scheme is a crucial social service. A useful, simple and well-written guide, setting out sample booklets and newsletters is *Pensions: promoting and communicating your scheme* (by Sue Ward, published by the Industrial Society Press, 1990, £16.95, ISBN 0-85290-472-X).

Statistics

Getting statistics in pensions is rarely a problem – getting useful ones is all but impossible. The government used to publish quarterly investment statistics about pension funds, but has discontinued them following substantial errors in their compilation. The National Statistics website does however have a wealth of information on pensions. UBS publish *Pension fund indicators* (020-7901 5137) analysing investments. The NAPF publishes an annual survey which shows what pension funds are doing now in certain abstruse areas – but fails to show trends or comparative figures. You can use their database by arrangement. A useful guide, really designed for use by actuaries, is the *Pensions pocketbook*, which comes out every year (NTC Publications / Hewitt Bacon & Woodrow, Farm Road, Henley on Thames, Oxfordshire RG9 1EJ (01491 411000), ISBN 1-84116-146-2). *Watson Wyatt statistics* is a nicely produced monthly digest of pensions statistics (Watson Wyatt Worldwide, Watson House, London Road, Reigate, Surrey RH2 9PQ 01737 241144, www.watson-wyatt.com). The Government Actuary has published his Eleventh Survey (*Occupational pension schemes 2000*,

HMSO, 2003, ISBN 0-9544972-0-1, £5.50 – which shows the time it takes to do these things!) (www.gad.co.uk). Aon publish a small booklet of annual statistics (www.aon.co.uk, 11 Devonshire Square, London EC2M 4YR 0800-279 5588)

Directories

The NAPF publishes a yearbook (NAPF, NIOC House, 4 Victoria Street, London SW1H ONX 020-7808 1300 www.napf.co.uk) for the moment only on their website, and the principal directory is *Pension funds and their advisers* (Alan Philip, AP Information Services, Marlborough House, 298 Regents Park Road, London N3 2UU 020-8349 9988 www.apinfo.co.uk 2004 ed £195). The same outfit also publishes the even larger *International pension funds and their advisers*. Local authority trustees (councillors and others) should have the *PIRC local authority pension fund yearbook*, (annual, PIRC, ISBN 0-904677-42-7, £115) and might turn to *Pension funds performance guide (local authority edition)* £250 (DG Publishing, 9 Carmelite Street, London EC4Y ODR www.pensionsperformance.com)

Investments

There is no good all round guide for beginners; however, *Pension fund indicators* is published annually by UBS (020-7901 5315); www.ubs.com /1/e/globalam/uk/institutional/publications gives a survey of the various sectors with good graphs and charts (sometimes over-complicated) and is the generally regarded main source.

Comparative surveys

If you are asked to compare benefits in your scheme with other schemes, you can commission a survey of your own surprisingly cheaply – the NAPF will run a search through its database, though you won't know the names of the other companies.

Management and administration

As yet there do not appear to be any useful guides to administration and management. But there is now a government website, www.pensionsatwork.gov.uk which suggests ways of improving workplace pensions; the site is designed mostly for HR and pensions managers.

Giving advice

It is usually very unwise to attempt to attempt to advise members of their options; the regulations are not very sympathetic to trustees. But if you are asked for a guide try Jonquil Lowe *Take control of your pension* (Which?, ISBN 0-85202-927-6 www.which.net £10.99). For handing out to pensioners, you could try *Your Rights* 2004-2005, *a guide to money benefits for older people* Sally West, ISBN: 0862423937, 176pp, April 2004, £4.99 (Age Concern, Department YR, Age Concern England, Astral House, 1268 London Road, London SW16 4ER, 020-8765 7200, less in bulk(www.ageconcern.org.uk). There is also *The directory of pre-retirement courses*, (Pre-Retirement Association, annual), which is self-explanatory. Rosemary Brown, *Good non-retirement guide* (annual) (Enterprise Dynamics ISBN 0-7494 4145 3 www.kogan-page.co.uk (£12.79) is comprehensive and readable.

Whether a member should top-up his pension is best left to others to advise; members can be referred to the not terribly helpful *FSA Guide to topping up your occupational pension*, (www.fsa.gov.uk/ consumer, free) together with fact sheets.

Sources

Websites

- www.trusteetoolkit.com
- www.trusteetutor.com
- www.trusteemasterclass.com
- www.pensionsadvisoryservice.org.uk
- www.pensions-pmi.org.uk
- www.pensionsregulator.gov.uk
- www.napf.co.uk
- www.engaged-investor.com
- www.pensionsgym.com
- www.trustnet.com
- www.pensionfundsonline.co.uk
- www.pensions-age.com
- www.globalpensions.com
- www.pensionsworld.co.uk
- www.ipe.com
- www.hedgeweek.com
- www.bfinance.co.uk

NOTES

Publications

- 'The Pension Trustee's Handbook', Robin Ellison, Thorogood, 2007

- 'Pensions and Investments', Robin Ellison, Tottel, 2008

- 'All You Need to Know About Being a Pension Fund Trustee', Andrew Freeman, Longtail, 2006

- 'Pension Fund Indicators 2007', UBS Global Asset Management

- 'Multi Asset Class Investment Strategy', Guy Fraser-Sampson, Wiley, 2006

- 'Bringing Private Equity into Focus', Blackrock Investment Management, 2007 (further details at www.blackrock.co.uk)

- 'Hedge funds and funds of hedge funds made simple: what a trustee needs to know', National Association of Pension Funds, 2005

- Corporate Bonds Made Simple, National Association of Pension Funds, 2002

- 'Private Equity and Venture Capital Made Simple', National Association of Pension Funds, 2000

- 'Swaps Made Simple', National Association of Pension Funds, 2005

- 'Fixed Income Derivatives Made Simple', National Association of Pension Funds, 2005

Index of advertisers

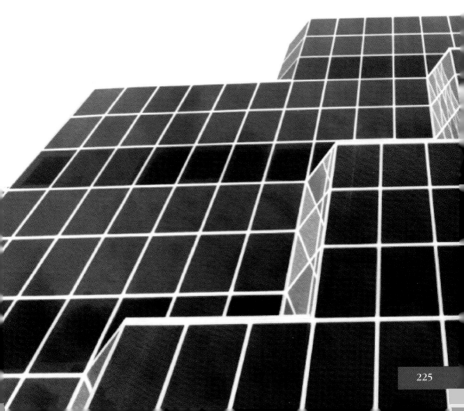

Index of advertisers

NOTES

Pension Trustee's Investment Guide – Free Copy Offer

In order to make the most of this book for you and your colleagues we would like to send a FREE COPY to your nominated colleague. Please provide the following details:

Your Name _____

Position _____

Company _____

Address _____

_____

Email address _____

Responsibilities _____

_____

Name of Colleague _____

Position _____

Company _____

Address _____

_____

Email address _____

Responsibilities _____

_____

Please return the form to: Geeta Chambers, Thorogood Publishing, 10-12 Rivington Street, London EC2A 3DU

Or email this information to:
Geeta.Chambers@thorogoodpublishing.co.uk